Embracing
the
Mystic Within

by Denise Iwaniw

The Temple Within llc
219 Glenview Court NE
Rockford MI 49341
www.templewithin.com

First Edition 2007©

ISBN: 0-9722002-3-1

Graphics: Wendy Mersman, Moon Designs, LLC.

Printed in the USA
Sentinel Printing Co.
St. Cloud MN 56304

Table of Contents

Part One

The Journey Begins

Preface

Dedication

Part Two

A Guide to Meeting the Mystic Within

Preface

At the very beginning of my life, I learned coincidences just don't exist. It was no coincidence that I was born in Augusta, Georgia and put up for adoption. It was no coincidence that the first family who adopted me decided it just wasn't going to work and gave me back to Social Services. I was still waiting for my "real" parents who were, in turn, in Michigan awaiting their next military destination. At the age of fifteen months, I finally met them when my father was posted to Ft. Gordon, Georgia. I've always told my mother she really belonged to me, but that I just had to take a few twists and turns to get to her. She was, after all, what I define as a real mother: the one who dried my tears, calmed my anxieties, pampered me through illnesses and celebrated my achievements as her own.

As the daughter of a career military man, twists and turns defined my life. Constant change was my life. At times it felt overwhelming and I longed for my own "home town." However, as I grew older, I realized these swoops and startles were critical to my overall journey both practically and spiritually.

Even as young as six, I remember seeing faces when I closed my eyes at night. While most were pleasant, some were gruesome. I can still vividly remember one old man, one of the first who came to me, floating just inches above my single bed one evening as I wrestled with sleep. Like the leftover from an old B horror film, he stared directly at me, struggling as if to tell me something. But he wasn't some childish conjuring; a bad dream captured fleetingly and turned into mythic proportions. He was palpable, a bulky man, with a broad face and a red bulbous nose, probably a leftover from many long nights with a bottle. Late 50s, I thought, thinning hair. His presence felt heavy, although the half-dozen times he came to me he was always disembodied. He was struggling to get through, to make the leap. He never spoke.

I never told my parents.

After all, I was six and scared to death. What could they, or any adult offer me, but the sweet hush-hush-there pats that only dismiss what is real and often what is really frightening?

My older playmates thought it strange that someone my age would be so preoccupied with ghosts. To this day, certain friends who knew me way back when never fail to remind me what a "weird little child" I was in their estimation. Those in spirit have always been a strong part of my life. I believe when you focus on something, all your energy flows into it, thus giving it power. Likewise, withholding energy means denying power.

That I was open to receiving such visitors, and that I in turn gave so much of myself over into the process, strengthened what was always as much a part of me and unquestionable as my green eyes. Perhaps this is why I appear so strong at funerals. I've always known that what we call death is really just a transition. Many have admired my strength in the face of a loved one's passing, but it truly wasn't what I would call strength. Rather it was a knowing that those we love are truly always with us and continue to guide us from a place we have yet to see.

Although I have experienced the presence of those in spirit throughout much of my life and watched dreams, both good and bad come to fruition, it wasn't until the summer of 1995 that I experienced my own personal awakening. Until this point, no one could tell me how or why such visions occurred.

During the course of my work on the manuscript for this book, I was asked countless times why I would write a book that could very well lead to endless scrutiny and skepticism. What could I possibly gain?

My answer has always been the same. It is my belief that all of us who occupy this life together are bound by something deeper than what we see concretely in front of us. Through the course of our daily lives, I feel we are touched in many ways by things we can't necessarily explain or prove in scientific terms. Those like myself have a heightened sensitivity to things that others cannot necessarily see or feel. Some call it psychic phenomena. I prefer not to think of it in scientific terms. Can I prove that my experiences have any scientific basis? No. I simply offer them, first and foremost, with sincere gratitude to the friends and family as well as my clients who have allowed me to share their experiences with you. Out of respect for their privacy, I have changed their names thoughout this book.

My hope is that by reading these pages, others may find comfort in the knowledge that they are not alone in their experiences, as I felt for many years of my life. This pageant which we call earth is but a drama, and what we call death is merely an end to a chapter in the book of our lives. Turning that page brings us to the life we originated from and will ultimately return to one day.

The essence of this book is devoted to my parents, Donn and Lois Cronk, who traveled countless miles to bring me home. To my beloved aunt, Mary Lou, I say,

"Even in spirit, you are still my favorite you-know-what."

-Denise

A Word from the Editor

Have you ever thought about writing a book?

With those words, uttered so casually over tuna salad and broiled chicken, my life took a 180-degree turn. Because they weren't typical lunch chatter: They were an open invitation, an offer.

Like many new opportunities, the chance to work with Denise has proven to be a double-edged sword. On the one hand, this collaborative effort has allowed me to spend up-close-and-personal time with a talented, gentle and truly incredible woman. On the other, every time I pick up a pen or schedule a lunch meeting to continue editing and interviewing, I plunge anew into the painful death of my own mother.

Like Denise, I believe there are no coincidences. As a former journalist, by definition, I should have been skeptical of Denise's gifts, of the very word, "psychic." But each day, I confront things in my work I neither understand nor can duplicate, and I am not dismissive of these. I think it's important to strip away what society conditions us to see or think or believe with what our hearts and our heads tell us, even when contradictions arise.

I do not share Denise's vision, true enough, nor even her calm and conviction in the face of grief and death. But Denise believes, shares these things with me, and I believe them because I believe her.

As Robert Heinlein wrote in the now classic "Stranger in a Strange Land," what harm is there in turning a (wo)man 180-degrees from everything else? No harm at all, I have found, unless that means turning your back on something or someone without fully hearing.

My contribution here is in memory of my mother, who in life would probably have been aghast at these chapters. I hope, with the transition she has now made, she is able to find comfort in them.

As ultimately, am I.

Mary Ann Sabo

"Your life is a gift from the Creator.
Your gift back to the Creator is what you do with your life."

Billy Mills, (1938-) Oglala Lakota Sioux, born and raised on Pine Ridge Reservation SD,
Gold Medal Winner at the 1964 Olympic Games in Tokyo, Japan

Part One
The Journey Begins

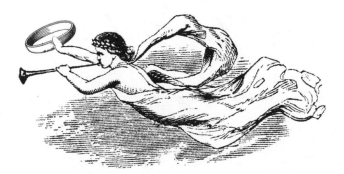

In the Beginning

It's easy for the mind to play tricks on the body and even easier for the body to convince itself it's being tricked. In the spring of 1996, my spiritual adviser echoed a question which others invariably get around to asking: How do I know for certain that the events, the visions and dreams, are real? Granted, I had had a number of small things happen over the course of a lifetime. So common are these I almost dismiss them as evidence. And too, most of the scenes played out in my mind. It's natural to wonder if something's real under such circumstances, or a product of fatigue, desire, grief or any of the other strong emotions, which can overtake and consume.

But one September evening in 1983 ended whatever lingering questions plagued me about my gift. That was the night my cousin Rick, who had killed himself just a few months before, came and sat down on the edge of my bed.

When it's in your mind, you wonder, after all. That is the nature of man.

But when you can actually feel someone sit down on the side of your bed, feel the mattress weighted down with his presence, then you know.

And it was then I knew.

A few months before my 21st birthday, I was drying dishes in my parents' kitchen, circling the brown stoneware plates methodically and thinking about getting ready to move into my own apartment.

I answered the phone on the second ring, but couldn't understand what the caller was saying. Laughing, I handed the receiver to my mother to see if she could decipher the voice.

"Who is this?" my mother asked, unable to identify the caller.

"WHAT?!" she screamed just seconds later. "Oh my God, Donn," she screamed for my father, before breaking down into wracking sobs. "It's Mary Lou."

Her next words would change our lives forever: "Rick's killed himself."

And then they were gone.

My brothers, Don and Tim, and I sat in stunned silence. Rick and I had just spoken the evening before. He was heading off to a party at a friend's. Rick was down, suffering through problems with his girlfriend, but we'd share details of our evenings, and agreed to talk again soon.

At 17, Don was only a year younger than Rick, but I don't feel the situation hit him after that call. At 11, Tim didn't understand the finality of Rick's action.

But I did. And my anger refused to allow tears.

How could you do that, I yelled at him in my mind. How could you go and just leave us without giving us a thought.

I saw him in my mind's eye then, a target to the selfish, enraged thoughts running through my head. Rick stood about 5'9", a good seven inches above my own petite frame. His oval face was framed by brown hair, which he kept trimmed meticulously. Rick owned beautiful eyes, greenish-blue and rather dreamy, long eyelashes most of my girlfriends' would have killed for. Bedroom eyes, you'd look at him and say. Those eyes were mischievous, but tempered by a warm and guileless smile. The whole package came wrapped in a stocky frame with muscled arms, the physique of a football center.

My parents were gone hours, days, it seemed, but when they finally returned, I locked myself in my room, talking alternately to my cat and to Rick. The anger softened into sadness as I realized my own selfishness in the matter, thought about whatever it was in his life that made him feel as if he was beyond help. My grief was compounded by the fact that, despite the closeness of our friendship, I had been powerless to help him, powerless to identify and alleviate some of his pain. I gave way to the tears, realizing not even my stern military upbringing would be able to hold them back.

After tucking my brothers into bed, my mother came to me and gave me the details. Her sister, Mary Lou, had noticed Rick was depressed, asked him if he wanted to talk. But Rick smiled and said, "No," settling into his bedroom to write two letters: one to his parents and one to his girlfriend. After he'd finished, Rick opened the bedroom window, got out his father's double-barreled shotgun and dragged his desk in front of the door.

Aunt Mary Lou and Uncle Bob were in the living room when they heard the blast. Despite Bob's emphysema, he bolted from his chair and broke through the door, my aunt a heartbeat behind. Mother said all that Mary Lou remembers was Rick's work boots.

Blood from the gunshot had somehow gotten underneath the framed picture of the varsity letter for football he had so proudly received. The senior picture of his team, with Rick grinning in the first row, was to be permanently stained. Mom and Dad were called, arrived, and began the process of righting the world again.

A process that would never be complete.

A day later, I sat on the white bedspread on one of the two twin beds in Rick's bedroom, talking to my cousin, Karen.

"Can you feel what's going on in this room?" I asked.

"Yes, you can feel it, too?" she said.

"It's dizzying," I said, "a whirlwind of energy."

"It's Rick's confusion," Karen replied. "We need to pray for him to follow the light."

Being an Army brat, I had never been around when someone had died. Whenever a relative had passed, one of my parents would fly back for the services. Rick's was to be my first funeral.

After the funeral mass, we followed the hearse to the cemetery. Surrounding us at the gravesite were dozens of floral arrangement: dish gardens with greenery, sprays of red and white carnations and fragrant red roses.

For my offering, I selected a dozen sky blue carnations for the feeling of lightness and healing that color gives off.

That evening, a terrible storm brought heavy rains and wind underscored by thunder. A friend suggested the flood was actually tears from Rick, sorrow over what he had done.

By morning, the storm had scattered all the carnations and vases and roses between the rough granite tombstones at the cemetery. All, that is, except for one.

Aunt Mary Lou phoned my mother early the next morning as she was preparing to go to her job as a cashier at the local grocery store.

"My God, Lois, you're not going to believe what you're going to see," Aunt Mary Lou breathed into the phone. "Bob and I were out there at 9 a.m., and you're not going to believe what you see."

"C'mon," my mother said to me, hanging up the phone, "We have to go out there."

Floral debris greeted us when we pulled up. Red and white carnations had flown the entire breadth of the tiny cemetery. A ring of roses had been knocked down, scattered. Flowers littered the entire carpet of green, as if a florist shop had exploded.

But standing next to the fresh mound of dirt, was a clear vase filled with the 12 blue carnations I had given Rick, right where they had been placed by the funeral director.

Untouched.

In September of that same year, I moved into a one-bedroom apartment I could finally call my own. Almost nightly, I dreamed of Rick.

In my dreams, he was just the same to me as he had been in life.

From a variety of standpoints, I needed to reassure myself Rick was fine. Rick had been looking at his life in such a black hole of anguish he truly saw no alternative but to end it. I needed confirmation, and I needed that message to come from Rick.

And one evening in September, I received the message I had been searching for.

Still exhausted from the funeral, I found myself retiring ever earlier each night. One evening, curled up in a favorite pink floral striped nightgown, I began reading Carl Jung's Memories and Dreams. I was really trying to focus, to make sense of the torrent of dreams I had been having but it was no use. About 9 p.m., I closed the book, clicked out the light, fluffed the pillows and prepared myself to sink into sleep.

It was then that I felt him.

I could feel someone at the foot of my bed, on the right side where males usually appear. I could feel someone sitting.

At first, I was frightened. I held my breath and tried to calm the thump-thump-thumping of my racing heart. My eyes were still adjusting to the darkness and I could not quite make out a shape, but the feeling of weight, of the springs sinking just a bit lower, was unmistakable.

All of a sudden, I was overcome by a sense of calmness, of peace. I realized my visitor was none other than Rick. I could feel the energy of his spirit, almost as if that energy was saying, "It's okay, it's just me." His voice was in my head, talking, talking.

We stayed that way a good minute which is a long time, when you're sitting in the dark with someone on the edge of your bed. I felt the weight being lifted, Rick removing himself from the edge of my bed. While I was sad that he was leaving again, I had been comforted by his visit.

"It's okay," he had told me. "I'm okay. I've found the Light. It's alright."

My fiancé' Steve and I began to make our wedding plans almost a year before the date we chose. There was champagne to buy and flowers to order, and other hoops to jump through as mandated by our church.

It was during one of our pre-marital counseling sessions that I found the courage to broach the subject of my dreams and extrasensory experiences with our parish priest. Steve excused himself for a bathroom break and, recognizing my chance, I jumped in.

"Father, I need to talk to you about something that's happened to me, and I'm hoping you can explain," I started, bracing myself in my chair.

"I'll try," he said.

"You remember my cousin Rick?" I asked him, before launching into the story about the flowers, about my dreams about Rick sitting on my bed. "And I know he was there," I concluded, scanning the priest's face to gauge a reaction.

"Are you sure you weren't just dreaming," he asked. "You had been reading a book."

"No, Father, I wasn't dreaming," I insisted. "I felt someone sit at the foot of my bed and then get up again."

The mild-mannered priest with the slight build and the thick glasses just looked at me, speechless.

"I've never encountered that in my life," Father replied. "It must be you were just having a dream because you wanted him there. Just leave it alone, my dear."

Talk about having the wind knocked out of your sails. If you can't confide in your parish priest, just whom can you talk to, I wondered. Steve returned to the room a moment later, and the topic turned to pre-marital sex – something our parish priest was obviously more comfortable discussing.

Although I would talk occasionally with Steve and with other family members, It would be another decade before I would broach the subject again with any "outsider."

A friend once asked why I was so deeply connected to dead people. My answer was simple: Because they're not really dead.

For as long as I can remember, I've had this inner knowing when someone has either died or was preparing to. That someone could either be close to me or removed from my life. I remember standing in the shower one morning when it came to me that the Marlboro man had died and he'd died of lung cancer. The irony of it all, I though, that such a handsome, rugged man would become a casualty of the very product he had come to represent. Later that day, my thought was confirmed by the news.

At other times, such knowing weighs heavier. I was lying in bed, dozing one morning, when the phone began to ring. "Uncle Bob is dead," I thought. "I don't want to hear it though, so I won't answer the phone."

Immediately I was flooded with images of the uncle I adored. His death would bring an end to the spaghetti-dinner birthday parties that had been a staple of my youth, the annual reading of "The Night Before Christmas," the singing of songs around the family warmth of our kitchen table.

The phone eventually fell silent.

About five minutes later, it started ringing again. I gulped, decided I might as well face what had happened and answered it.

Steve was on the other end, asking why I hadn't picked up just minutes ago when my mother called.

"Because Uncle Bob is dead and I didn't want to hear it," I said matter-of-factly.

Steve confirmed what I already knew. My uncle had passed in his sleep just hours before. It would be this same uncle who would, years later, prepare me for the death of a woman I loved very deeply.

The absence of so many dear family members could not help but throw small shadows over my wedding day in October of 1985. Even in the months of planning which preceded the celebration, Rick and my Uncle Bob and others would occasionally make their absence known, surfacing in memories and what ifs?

The evening of our wedding brought hundreds of friends and relatives to help us celebrate. During the reception, my Aunt Mary Lou walked up to me and said: "We all know how much you wanted Rick to be here with you. Apparently, he does too."

She extended her hand to me. Cradled in it was Rick's class ring, a blue sapphire with an eagle emblazoned on one side and a football on the other. We thought he had given it to an old girlfriend, and the family despaired it was irretrievable after his death.

For two years, we searched. Every nook and cranny, every possible hiding place, but no ring.

We finally resigned ourselves that Rick's ring was either lost or with the girlfriend. But on the very morning of our wedding, the father of our best man who happened to be the high school principal was cleaning out some old lockers when he put his hand on one of the top shelves and found something shiny.

To his astonishment, and to ours, it was Rick's class ring, his name in careful script curving around the inside of the band. Knowing what it would mean to my aunt, he brought the ring with him to the wedding.

He had no idea how much it would mean to the bride.

* * * *

My parents owned a two-bedroom cottage on Pettibone Lake, a small grayish place. The front was lined with windows, huge eyes overlooking a large yard that stretched until the beach began. Oaks bordered the right. Another small cottage was to the left, and it was a quick 100-yard scamper to the white dock and beyond it, the cool inviting blue of the lake. This was our family's rustic weekend get-away complete with a two- seater outhouse.

Swimming and boating filled each glorious day that summer of 1991. My father had dug a burn pit, and each evening we would pack it with wood and head out onto the lake for a pontoon ride. By the time we returned, the entire pit would be blazing, and we would swap jokes and stories, often lingering into the early hours of the morning. My mother and her sister, Mary Lou, would keep the fire blazing long after we had all retired, spinning their quiet, sisterly webs.

Aunt Lou, as everyone called her, even children at the library where she worked, was a petite woman with a slim build. I remember her grayish-green eyes, eyes that she'd passed on to her son, Rick. She was a spotless woman, always dressed in a smart looking pair polyester pants with flats to match. She sported a delightful sense of humor, a consuming passion for Stephen King novels, and a love of the water. When she wasn't cruising the lake in a pontoon, she could be found sitting in one of the lawn chairs, reading.

Or playing with my son Dane, who was two at the time. The pair loved one another fiercely. He followed his Aunt Lou around the cottage like a small, faithful puppy, energetic and loving. She reciprocated with warm smiles and arms always eager to embrace him. They often danced around the campfire before bedtime, forging a bond that would last beyond this lifetime. She would croon her favorite song to him, while she danced, Patsy Cline's "Crazy."

"Crazy, I'm crazy for feeling so lonely," she would murmur into Dane's cheek while they danced.

As is the way with all good summers, it seemed that one would last forever. One evening, watching the flames dance and play with the shadows of my family gathered around the bonfire, I was struck by a sudden sadness. Not the inevitable melancholy which embraces a slowly fading season, but the surety of knowledge that this would be the last summer we would ever enjoy this same way.

My mother received a phone call that autumn which again changed our lives irrevocably.

"Aunt Lois," came the pleading voice of my cousin, "get over here."

My mother raced to her sister's side and found Mary Lou coughing up blood.

Days later, the doctor confirmed our family's worst fears: lung cancer. My aunt, a life-long smoker, laid aside the cigarettes when she heard, steeled herself for the endless doctor visits and radiation treatments now outlined to preserve her future.

One or two mornings a week, I would take my aunt for her radiation therapy before work. During the half-hour trip, we talked about how well the treatments were going, how at 59 she was too young to die, how surely she could beat this disease.

The following summer, we returned to the weekending at the lake. Chemotherapy was added to Aunt Lou's radiation sessions, but she often joined the family, reveling in the sunshine. I can still see my mother brushing her sister's hair by the lake, watching the thin, brown strands fall out by the fistful.

"My hair-care program's going to be pretty easy in a few weeks," quipped Aunt Lou, her graceful humor settling the situation.

We bought her bright pink baseball caps and turquoise turbans, colorful headgear to cover the results of the chemo. One elegant white turban of which she was particularly fond always puzzled me: did she look more like Nora Desmond or like the resident of an ashram I'd wonder, whenever I saw her. It made us both laugh.

At this point, my Uncle Bob visited me in a dream one night while I was sleeping. I saw him sitting in a brown velvet rocker and when he noticed me, he looked up and shook his head. He spoke, although his lips didn't move.

"She's not going to make it," he told me. "She's coming with me."

That was it then. I had already long learned to trust my dreams, but this was one I couldn't bear to consider. While I tried to be optimistic on the outside, deep, deep inside I knew the inevitable truth which I never shared with anyone.

As Aunt Lou grew weaker, her daughter and my mother became her central caregivers. The steady rhythm of the oxygen machine became white noise underpinning the endless hours of cooking, cleaning and comforting that went into each day. They took turns spending the night so Aunt Lou would never be alone. The rest of the women in the family devoted their weekends to tending to Aunt Lou, giving a little respite to my cousin and my mother.

At the beginning, my aunt refused to use the hospital bed we'd gotten for her. She wisecracked, "Once I get into that bed, I won't leave the house without being in it, I just know." Aunt Lou told her daughter she wasn't afraid to die, she just wasn't ready yet. On those nights and weekends when we converged on the house, she would gather us around her bed, encouraging us to tell and retell the funny stories from our youth. But little by little, in small ways at first, we noticed she began slipping away from us. Although meticulous about her personal grooming, one day she asked me not to bother filing and buffing her fingernails. "It's just too painful," she said.

My son, Dane, used to run to his Aunt Lou, lunging at her and wrapping her in a bear hug. But one afternoon, he began noticing the turbans, the tubes that tied her to the oxygen tank, the unsteady way she sat in her recliner, and hesitated. You could read in her eyes just how much that reluctance tore at her.

In the last few days, my aunt began to call out to her husband, Bob. We knew that as her time here grew shorter, my uncle came close to reassure her. Just two nights before she died, my aunt called my mother into her room and took her hand. Aunt Lou told her she could see their parents, my grandparents and her children who had passed before her, just waiting for her to join them.

Although I was in the living room, I remember feeling like I was surrounded by people I couldn't see. There was an expectancy in the air, a very warm energy, almost like the feeling when you're driving to your grandmother's and you know she's going to meet you at the front door. And when she does meet you, she'll be waving and yelling and just as happy for the reunion as you are.

"Can you feel this?" I said to my cousin.

"I can," she replied.

Her affirmation was echoed by the visiting nurse from hospice, who said, "It's my belief the closer we come to death, the nearer our loved ones come to help us cross over."

My aunt sank further into silence as we watched her body physically shutting itself down. For days she was nearly comatose, unable to utter a word. On what was to be Aunt Lou's last day on earth, I entered her bedroom to the cheery question, "Hey, did I ever tell you that you're my favorite you-know-what?"

"Yes, you did," I said, surprised at her sudden fervor.

"And does your mother know I love her?" she asked.

"Yes, she does," I said.

"And do you know I love you?"

"Yes," I replied, that monosyllable nearly catching in my throat. "Promise me, when it's my turn, you'll be the one to greet me when I get to the other side."

She smiled weakly and said, "Yes, I will."

I wasn't with her that evening when she passed, but I was not surprised to get the call. Her lungs kept filling up, yet she was waiting to hear that her new grandson had arrived before letting go. She died an hour after hearing the good word from her son, one soul just coming into the world, another leaving it.

As I climbed the stairs into her house, calmness and peace washed over me. The steady breathe-breathe-breathe of the oxygen machine was replaced by a tranquility I will never forget. I sat beside her on the bed, stroking Aunt Lou's hair over and over again. She had been so proud it had finally agreed to grow back in and such a beautiful and pure white!

"Your battle was long," I whispered. "It was visually the most horrific thing I've ever witnessed, yet spiritually, the most beautiful. You fought valiantly."

"Remember, you have promised to meet me on the other side when it's my turn to cross over."

I sat with my family that night and wrote her obituary. We finished about midnight. And then we all shared a beer.

Aunt Lou stayed nearby, though, letting us know she was with us in very definite ways. That's how she came to visit Dane, who was not quite three when his great aunt died. Like all small children, Dane was confused by the concept of death. He broke it down to the simplest of ideas: He had grown accustomed to seeing her each and every day of his life, and then suddenly, she was nowhere to be found. I imagine that's how he saw death from his tiny viewpoint.

Over the next few months, Dane became withdrawn. I tried everything to help him snap out of his depression, but to no avail. At my wit's end, I finally pleaded with my aunt to come to Dane in a dream and let him know she was all right.

Four days later, I woke to hear Dane sobbing but when I approached his bed, I could see he was sound asleep. He cried for several more minutes before laying his head back on the pillow, never once waking.

When he finally came to breakfast that morning, I asked, "Honey, did you have a bad dream this morning that made you cry?"

"No, Mommy. I was talking to Aunt Lou," he said, spooning brown sugar on his oatmeal.

"What did she say to you?" I asked.

"She said, 'I'm okay Dane. I love you and miss you.'" And with that, Dane became himself once again.

The next year, my parents built a new house on Pettibone Lake, a stylish 3-bedroom ranch, boasting indoor plumbing, landscaping lights and lots of hanging flowers and window boxes. We gathered together on the first night, and conversation turned to Aunt Lou and how much she would have loved this new place.

A moment of silence fell into the room, as each of us fell into thoughts of Mary Lou. "Crazy, I'm crazy for feeling so lonely," began Patsy Cline's thin, lonesome voice over my mother's radio.

Overcome, she stepped outside. The rest of us knew Auntie was just saying she did enjoy their new home.

"I'm crazy for crying and crazy for trying and crazy for loving you."

As I said, there's no such thing as a coincidence.

The Awakening

he following week I purchased a book by Sonia Choquette called The Psychic Pathway. It would prove to be a turning point in my life. As I read her book, all of the metaphysical events which had occurred during my life started to gain some meaning. By looking at her photo on the back of her book, I knew she was the one who could help me. Both my dear friend, Colleen, and my husband, Steve, told me Sonia looked like she could be my sister. My daughter, Elyse, asked me if it was a picture of me on the back of the book. I felt this was confirmation of my feeling.

The first week of July I phoned Sonia's office and asked to make an appointment.

I was told that she was booked for a year solid and had a waiting list. Her secretary asked me if I would like a referral. I told her no. I then proceeded to tell her about my latest revelation and how I felt from looking at Sonia's face that I was being guided in her direction. The woman told me that she had heard that from others as well, then asked me if it was okay to put me on hold. Within a few minutes, Sonia's secretary was back on the phone. She told me that Sonia would like to see me at 1 p.m. the following Tuesday. I agreed to the time and date.

Immediately, I went to see Colleen. I asked her if she had the following Tuesday free to travel to Chicago. She asked me why and I told her. She said she would go with me. She knew how important it was to me.

Perhaps it is because we were both raised in Catholic families, but both of us were a little apprehensive about going to see a "psychic." The term alone is intimidating simply because of all the negative connotations that go with it. Add to that view that most religious organizations have of such phenomena and you feel as though you are treading on the brink of something very evil. Soon I would learn that nothing is further from the truth.

My parents raised me and my brothers to value every religion. Even if this respect was not mutual, we were taught that everyone worships in his or her own way and that was to be respected. My way was with deep devotion to the Holy Mother. I have always felt her presence in my life whenever I felt at the end of my rope. She has always lead me safely through and I knew she would be with us as we traveled to Chicago. On the morning of our trip, I asked for a sign that I was doing the right thing.

When I picked up Colleen, she told me that she had a message to give me. She wasn't sure how or why, but she woke up that morning knowing that she had to tell me something. She then said that Sonia would tell me something very upsetting during our meeting. However, it was something that has already happened. I was to think it through and then I would realize what she was actually telling me.

Not too far off Lakeshore Drive on the north side of Chicago, we found Sonia's home without any trouble. With time to pass, we stopped and had lunch at a restaurant just down the street. We saw people of every race, creed and age walking by the restaurant window. Old women walked down the streets with groceries, while Arabic men and women walked with their families. Soon, it was time to head for my appointment.

As we drove, we marveled at the wealth of humanity roaming around the streets. Hindu women in beautiful saris, African-American families out for a walk on a warm and sunny day. Mom-and-pop hardware and grocery stores lined the streets as did

Lebanese restaurants and small dress shops. Being an Army brat, I felt right at home amongst all these different people.

Meeting Sonia was a little frightening. I already knew in my heart of hearts what Sonia was going to tell me, but I needed external confirmation before I went on to tell my family and friends.

In western culture psychics and clairvoyants have always been portrayed as wild Gypsies in a late-night movies hunched over a crystal ball. They're not ever shown in an ordinary light. They are never shown as a spiritual gift, but as an oddity.

As I approached Sonia's street, Colleen said, "Denise, there is your sign." There, imbedded in the corner of a brown brick building at the end of Sonia's street was a tile mosaic of the Blessed Mother. In shades of red and royal blue and wearing halos of gold were the faces of Mary and the Christ child. Once again, the Holy Mother was guiding my journey.

As we pulled up to Sonia's two-story brownstone home, we were met by an open porch decorated with bright red geraniums and an assortment of vividly colorful annuals.

Sonia greeted us at her front door and led us to her sitting room. I was struck by the fact that her home very closely resembled my own: Oak floors, pieces of art hanging on ivory walls, painting in oranges and reds and yellows. Her home was purposely decorated in the colors of the first three chakras, bringing a grounding and balancing force into her home. I felt very comfortable, like I was sitting in my own home. The gentle, meditative music of sitars played as we waited for Sonia to ready herself for my reading.

I was nervous, waiting for her to confirm something I'd known about myself. I knew that I would have to tell people. The anticipation of the reactions I might receive worried me. While Colleen talked about how much she disliked the music, I sat back on the sofa and quietly waited.

Moments later, Sonia took me to her reading room. I walked into a room almost identical to that of my own living room at home. It was filled with large bookcases loaded with literature, family portraits and various treasures accumulated during a lifetime. The icons of the Holy Mother, however, immediately grabbed my attention. There, on the small round reading table, sat two small icons perched on stands.

When I commented on them, Sonia told me that she never does a reading without the guidance of St. Mary. Having been raised in a Catholic family herself, she shared my reverence for the Blessed Mother.

After I sat down at her reading table, Eastern music playing lightly in the background, she asked me for my gold watch so that she could gather information about me from the personal energy that my watch contained. The first question Sonia asked me was whether I had ever designed a set of tarot cards. She sensed that I was highly artistic. I explained that I had been taught that things of that nature were demonic. As she brought out her own beautiful deck of cards, she chuckled and told me the story behind the Cathars and the use of the tarot as a divination tool. She explained that by using tarot, she was able to connect with her own spirit guides for answers. She then asked me to shuffle her tarot cards. This was the first time I'd ever touched a tarot deck. I wasn't sure if I was crossing into dark territory. My mind was playing into one of the fears and stereotypes I had grown up with. Gypsies wearing bright red bandana head scarves and large gold earrings turning over the death card or the hangman.

Sonia could sense my uneasiness as I shuffled the cards. She told me to relax. I continued to shuffle the deck and became more relaxed. I watched her intently as she used her brass I Ching coins, throwing them down, and taking down the formation for later deciphering.

I handed the deck back to her, anxious to see what would happen next and praying that she didn't turn over the dreaded Death card. I watched her as she placed the cards in a configuration on the table. After laying them out in a straight row, she asked me to choose five cards and then hand them to her.

Sonia asked me if I was prepared to make a great change in my lifestyle. I told her that yes, I was. I had traveled nearly 200 miles to see her because I knew I had to make changes. I told her that I was at a turning point in my life and I knew she was the one who would help me around the bend.

Quite bluntly, she then asked me if I knew that I was a psychic sensitive. It was the first time I had ever heard that phrase. I told her that I didn't know what it was called but that recently this "gift" had begun to feel like a curse hanging over my head. Whatever it was, it was draining my energy and leaving me exhausted every night. She looked at me very seriously and said: "Denise, this is a gift from God. It is not a curse. You have neglected the yearnings of your soul for too long now. It is time to start honoring who you really are. I know that you are highly creative and have witnessed many miracles in your life. You are like a great big antenna and every time you are in a relaxed state, every Tom, Paul and Harry who wants to communicate to someone on the earth plane, tries to go through you."

She explained to me that my own soul chose to come into this world and experience rejection through being given up at birth for adoption. It was a lesson I chose to learn in this lifetime. Likewise, I had already chosen my parents prior to birth. She asked me what the delay was in getting to them. I explained that I had been adopted once prior to connecting with my mom and dad. "Oh," she said, "By the way, the reason you chose a military family is due to the fact that your sensitive soul needed the strict atmosphere." I was stunned.

When I asked Sonia why she had agreed to see me with such a long list of people wanting to see her, she told me that her spirit guides told her that it was important for her to help me. When I commented on how three people thought her jacket photo resembled me, she laughed and said, "Of course we look alike, we are of the same spiritual family, Denise."

Her words brought peace to my soul. It felt as though the weight of the world had been lifted off my shoulders. Finally, someone was able to help me! Sonia continued to explain that there was a reason for all of this and that my true purpose on earth is that of a psychic counselor; a counselor for the spirit.

Sonia stood up and walked over to one of the large bookcases in the room, retrieving a large round ball of black obsidian and said, "Hold this." It was smooth and cool to the touch. "I want you to get a piece of obsidian", she said, because it absorbs psychic energy. Before you go to sleep, ask your guides in spirit to protect you from all negativity. You've been giving permission to all these squatters, and you've allowed it to happen. Even Jesus always encouraged people to stand up on their own two feet; he didn't carry them all on his back."

For two weeks prior to seeing Sonia, I kept hearing a word like Enid or Enoch with my inner ear. I asked Sonia if she could tell me who my spirit guide was. A huge smile lit up her face and she replied "Denise, you are being guided by a very old Celtic soul by the name of Enid. She is very wise and is here to help you always." I said, "Well, I was certainly close," and proceeded to tell her what I had been hearing prior to our meeting in Chicago.

Sonia explained that I have many spirit guides and that as I progressed spiritually, they would come to me, each with a different purpose. Enid's purpose is that of a master guide. She is the spiritual being who would see to it that the correct teachers and subsequent guides that I needed would come to me at the proper time.

I told Sonia that I had begun reading books about the psychic medium, George Anderson, and others like him. She was very adamant when she told me to quit reading those books. "It's time to quit being voyeuristic, Denise. You are capable of doing these same things. Drop the business classes you are taking and go back to art class. Get in touch with your true self. You were put on this earth as a psychic counselor to help people!"

She then went on to explain that because I am a psychic sensitive, I feel the pain and joy that others feel with equal intensity. Unless I started acknowledging this and began taking care of myself, my health would continue to suffer. I needed to learn how to screen it. "Unfortunately, not all spiritual energy is positive," she said. You want to avoid those entities at all times."

Then came the disturbing question. "Denise, is one of your children handicapped?"

"No," was my reply.

"Yes, one of them is handicapped," she said.

I told her that with the exception of an earache here and there, both of my children were perfectly healthy. Despite this, she told me that she could see quite clearly that one of my children had been in some sort of accident and was going through therapy. However, after a period of therapy, she told me this child would heal completely and eventually catch up to others of his own age. I was dumbfounded and very worried. because she had been so accurate with every other revelation. Throughout the final period of our meeting, this thought kept haunting me.

When our session finally came to an end, I thanked her for her time and insight. She told me to just think about the things she had said to me during our time together. She would send her love and prayers with my friend and me as we journeyed home. "Now, go out and do what God intended for you to do!" were her final words.

Once in the car, and safely back on Lakeshore Drive, Colleen asked me what Sonia had said to upset me. I told her about our conversation about my children. Then she reminded me of her message earlier that day. It was something that had already happened, Colleen had said; think it through and it will come to you.

Together we thought it over. As we did, it suddenly dawned on me that Sonia was indeed talking about one of my children, my godson. He had been in a horrible accident and was indeed going through therapy. He had suffered a terrible bruise on his brain and was still recovering. When I later told this to my godson's mother, she got tears in her eyes and said: "See what a special bond you have with my son. I knew I chose the right Godmother for him!" Months later she called to tell me that her son's teacher had informed her that within the next school year he would advance with children in a regular classroom setting. Sonia was right again.

When I returned home late that night, I woke my husband up to tell him what had happened. He listened intently, and then asked me if I felt she had helped me. Without a doubt, the answer was yes.

I then asked Steve to close his eyes and tell me what he saw. He described a black space with little bright spots like stars. "Is that all you see?" I said.

He replied "Yes. Why, what do you see?"

So I closed my eyes and began to describe all the faces. One in particular of an older black man with gray hair and a hat on his head. He reminded me of Frederick Douglass. Along with that vision was a black stagecoach rolling across my inner screen.

"I never knew you saw all those things at night," said Steve.

I replied, "And I never knew that everyone else *didn't* see things when they shut their eyes."

Then, as Sonia had instructed, I prayed to the Lord and my guardian angel to give me rest and protect me from all negativity as I slept. I had a very restful night. The first one in a long time.

Visitations

The hour that I spent with Sonia changed my life. It altered my outlook on myself and those around me. The words, "Denise, this is a gift from God," have stayed with me since. What a wonderful feeling. Having heard those words, I knew it was now up to me to find out how I was supposed to use this "gift" that had been entrusted to me.

In August of 1995, I began to have the first of what I call spiritual visitations. Although I had been experiencing them all my life, this was the first time I actually knew what was happening.

On a particularly hot August afternoon, I was sitting at my boss' desk, updating his files. When I went to reach for his gold pen to take down a message, I had a very strange feeling. As I looked up from his walnut desk, I could see his eldest daughter standing in front of me, surrounded by a beautiful blue light. Six years prior, she had passed away in a car accident, leaving two small children and a husband. Although I didn't know her all that well, she had a very distinct voice that I have never forgotten. Without moving her lips, I could hear her say: "Denise, please be sure to tell my children that I'm okay. Please, Denise, will you tell them that I'm with them always?" I could feel the desperation in her voice and at the same time, the relief of getting her message through to me. I was stunned. I could clearly see her and hear her, yet I wondered if my imagination was just getting the best of me.

Because the experience was so vivid and overwhelming, on my way to lunch that day I asked Colleen what she thought of this ordeal. She replied very simply, "Tell her you will deliver the message to her father and then do it."

"This is absurd," I replied.

"No. She has asked you to do this for her and now it is up to you to follow through for her," she said.

As Colleen and I ate Chinese food, I could hear this voice over and over repeating the same question. Eventually, I interrupted Colleen as we tried to converse. I felt as though I was having a three-way conversation! When I told Colleen this, she encouraged me to deliver the message. I felt a little foolish, however, I replied out loud "Okay, I promise to give your message to your father."

A flood of sadness and relief washed over me. Not mine, but that of a mother who was finally able to break through the veil of this life and the next to reassure her family of her continuing love and guidance.

Despite my promise, I have to admit that I was a bit reticent to tell my boss. Although we had touched on the subject of spiritual phenomena before, this was my first attempt at delivering a message such as this. Having great hunches and intuition is one thing. Delivering a message from the other side is quite another.

A week later when he came back from vacationing with his wife and two grandchildren, I finally decided to broach the subject. I started out by asking him how his trip to Gettysburg was, and then proceeded to ask him if the oldest of his grandchildren, his grandson, ever asked about his mother.

He replied that, "Yes, as he gets older, he asks more questions."

"What do you tell him when he asks about her?" I asked.

He replied "I tell him she earned the right to be in the place she is. Why do you ask?"

Very nervously, I said: "I know you don't think I'm crazy, and what I'm about to tell you may sound crazy, but it did happen. As I was sitting at your desk last week, I picked up your gold pen and could clearly see and hear your daughter. I've made a promise to give you the following message. Your daughter wants you to tell her children that she is okay and is always with them."

He stood in his office doorway and tried to digest what I had just told him. I asked him if he was okay and he replied "Yes, I'm fine."

"I hope you believe me," I said. This really did happen and I certainly would never say anything to upset you."

With tears in his eyes he replied: "Yes, I do believe you. My daughter gave me the gold pen that you picked up. It was a birthday gift." With that, he left the office for a few minutes.

Later that day I again asked him if I had upset him.

He told me, "No."

"In fact, he said, it makes me feel good."

"Then my mission has been accomplished," I replied.

After this experience, I began looking for someone who could give me some additional insight into this ability. Going to someone within my own church didn't seem like an option. Because of the response I received so many years earlier, I was certain I would again face the "it must have been a dream" point of view. I prayed each day that God would keep me on my true path.

With my friend Wendy, I began going to spiritual development classes at a Spiritualist church. My weekly visits to this small white chapel would further change my spiritual life.

Since I was raised to respect all religious traditions, this didn't seem like a strange idea. In fact, it was a wonderful feeling to be sitting in a room with people who were having like experiences and to be able to talk freely about them. We were all there to learn about these gifts together.

The evening of my very first class, I learned something that I will never forget. Our instructor asked us to turn in the Bible to 1st Corinthians Chapter 12. There, right before my eyes, was the biblical interpretation of what I had been experiencing all my life. "How could this have escaped me for 32 years?" I wondered. I went home and read it over and over again.

I continue to find a tremendous amount of serenity in those words.

Over the next several months, I was taught how to communicate more clearly with my spirit guides and how to interpret their communications more accurately. I learned to fine tune my clairaudient and clairvoyant abilities, which allow me to hear and see those in spirit. I became even more aware of Enid's presence in my life. Through sight and sound, we began to communicate with one another more easily.

I am forever grateful for my learning experience at the Spiritualist Church. The members were gracious and very supportive of me as I continued my quest for knowledge.

* * * *

Despite this, I still longed to find someone within my own Catholic faith that could help me continue my journey. My heart yearned to know that the church I had been baptized and confirmed in would not reject me. As I searched for that person, I began to experience the fullness of my spiritual gifts on a regular basis.

On October 18, 1995 I had a vision of a car accident while I was sitting at my office desk. On my inner screen of vision, I could see a small red car with a dented hood. It looked as though the hood had been pushed up in some way. I could see trees around a car with no one inside. I asked if this was my husband's small red car. Suddenly, I could see the word Neon, and knew it was the car owned by Colleen's fiancé, Brad.

Since I didn't see anyone injured inside the car, I kept this vision to myself. One morning, about a week later, Colleen told me that Brad had just called her because he had been in an accident. He decided to take an alternate route to work that morning and ended up hitting a deer. When I asked her what portion of the car had been damaged, she told me that it was the front end. The hood had been bent and pushed up. When I saw Brad's car a few days later at their rehearsal dinner, it looked exactly as I had been shown.

The following month, I had a dream about an air crash in the Middle East that involved a military aircraft of some sort. The airplane had Middle Eastern writing along its side. I could fee the percussion of the blast as I sat in a pickup truck on a military base. As the windows blew out of the truck, I leaned over the seat to avoid the shards of glass. I then climbed out of the demolished pickup to see if I could help any of the people who had been aboard the ill-fated plane. A field littered with arms, legs and torsos that were covered in pieces of royal blue cloth greeted me. There was no one there for me to save. One week later, a Jordanian military plane crashed. There were no survivors.

Being aware of events that may potentially take place and yet having no power to change the outcome is sometimes very frustrating. I've come to realize that everything that happens in our lives happens for a purpose. Each of our experiences is significant in this lifetime. They are given to us as a chance to learn something new or to move past something old.

I have a dear friend from Texas who follows the teachings of a Hindu Avatar by the name of Meher Baba. He has always been a friend that I could talk to about these things. Never judgmental, he is always willing to give me the view of Eastern religion with regard to the events happening in my life. He is a great source of knowledge and spiritual comfort.

It was in the autumn of 1995 that he stopped by my office to tell me of his father's passing. During the course of our conversation, I could clearly see a black Bible adorned with a simple white cross on its leather cover. A profusion of white roses also accompanied this scene. I asked Chuck if his father was a Christian minister. He told me that while he was not an ordained minister, he mother had described his father as a "minister to his friends" during her eulogy to more than 300 of his friends and relatives.

As Chuck went on to talk about the events surrounding his father's death and memorial service, I could see a young boy in an outdoor setting with a beautiful golden retriever at his side. When I relayed this vision to Chuck, he told me his family has a photograph of his father just as I had described. I told my friend that I felt his father was a peace and doing just fine. Chuck was happy to hear this and thanked me for telling him what I saw.

Later that same week, as my boss stood in front of my filing cabinet I could see a Mason's symbol over his left shoulder. It felt as though it was a father figure trying to get my attention.

When I asked Paul if his father was a Mason, he said "No, but my father-in-law was. Why?" As he was talking, I could see fresh-cut peach and yellow roses and I could hear "These are for Eleanor." "Who is Eleanor?" I asked. With a very surprised look on his face, Paul replied, "Eleanor is my mother-in-law." I then saw a beautiful flower garden and asked Paul if Eleanor grew flowers. He told me that she does indeed grow flowers at her home in California. I asked him if it was customary for his father-in-law to give his wife roses. Paul responded by saying that his father-in-law loved his wife dearly and gave her flowers frequently. I told Paul what I was seeing and hearing. He asked me what it all meant. I smiled and told him his father in law, Paul, was sending his love to Eleanor. The flowers represented his undying love and affection for his wife.

As I spoke to Paul further, I could feel a shortness of breath and heaviness in my chest. Often times, those that have passed will indicate to me the manner in which they crossed over by having me experience it. I asked Paul if his father-in-law transitioned from a lung-related illness. He then told me that Paul had died from lung cancer.

It is a wonderful feeling to be able deliver a message such as this one from Paul to Eleanor. It is a great comfort to know our loved ones who have crossed over are still connected to us by the unbreakable bonds of love.

During and shortly after meditation is when I often find myself visited by those in spirit. Being in such a relaxed state, and having cleansed my mind of the hustle and bustle of the day, I am clearly more receptive to spirit.

Many times I am asked if I can assist someone in contacting a loved one on the other side. While many that have crossed over are very excited and willing to come in contact with those on the earth plane, for various reasons, others are not. Always before and after meditation, I ask the Creator to be with me in all I do. Such was the case on the beautiful, autumn afternoon of November 22, 1995.

As I sat in lotus position on the floor, I could see a beautiful young African-American woman in front of me. She had a flawless complexion and an exquisite smile. Her hair was covered by a blue bandana knotted in the front. She had a warm-hearted countenance and a wonderfully vibrant aura surrounding her. As I looked into her lovely brown eyes, I sensed she had a message that she wanted me to deliver.

I asked her name. I heard and saw the name "Anna." Do you have a message for me to give someone?" I asked. Her reply was a gentle "Yes." At this point she faded from my sight. The following day she present herself to me once again. This time she was accompanied by another African-American woman with short black hair. She reminded me of the actress, Cicely Tyson. When I asked her name I heard the reply "Annie," and saw the name spelled out in luminescent white letters. I was confused. Because the names were so similar, I wasn't sure that I heard the names correctly. I asked the questions once more and again saw both names clearly, Anna and Annie.

"Who is this message for?" I asked. "Wendy," was the response. "What is it you would like me to tell her?" I inquired.

Together, Ann and Annie showed me the following scene. Both of them were standing on either side of an older African-American gentleman wearing worn denim coveralls. He was holding an old wooden shovel while standing at the foot of a fresh grave site. The year 1922 was etched into the granite headstone. I could hear the words "Granny will be passing soon. Please tell Wendy we will be there to help her pass over."

The following day I asked my friend Wendy if she had a beautiful female relative by the name of Anna, who may have worn a navy blue bandana on her head. "No," was Wendy's response. I then asked her if she had any female relatives by the name of Annie who resembled Cicely Tyson. Again, Wendy's response was a confused, but simple "no."

Together we tried to figure out who these two women were. Because she could not identify with them, I did not proceed with the message. I thought perhaps I had misunderstood who the message was intended for.

Throughout my experiences as a medium, I have discovered that until I am able to deliver a message or "complete a mission," as I call it, those in Spirit wishing to make contact will stay at my side. This was the case with Annie and Anna. Both insisted that their message was for my friend, Wendy. Wendy, however, did not make the connection until four days later.

As I walked past Wendy's office, she very excitedly waved me over to her desk. With an astonished look on her face, she asked me to sit down for a moment.

"What was the name of the woman who appeared to you wearing a dark blue bandana?"

"She told me her name was Anna," I replied.

Wendy threw her hands up in the air and said "Why didn't I know this? I should have known it!" She continued, "Two weeks ago, my great grandmother, Anna passed away. Until her funeral, no one ever saw her hair because she kept it up in a blue rag that was tied in the front!" Wendy then asked "What was the name of the other woman?"

"Annie," was my response.

At that moment, Wendy picked up the phone and called her grandmother. Granny, as she fondly called her, had been living with Wendy for the past nine years. Wendy felt certain that Annie must be related to both Anna and Granny. When Granny answered the phone, Wendy asked her if she had any relatives by the name Annie. Granny responded by saying that she did have a deceased cousin by that name.

When Wendy asked if Annie resembled Cicely Tyson, Granny replied "Yes, she did look very much like Ms. Tyson."

"Why all this sudden fuss over my family?" Granny asked. Wendy responded that she had been talking to a friend about her family and just wanted some general information.

Wendy then asked me what it was that Annie and Anna wanted her to know. I told Wendy that these two women were in the company of an older African-American gentleman with a gray beard. I told her that he was wearing faded coveralls and that I got the impression that he was her Grandfather, Granny's husband. Wendy told me that yes, her Grandfather had passed several years prior and that he did wear coveralls because he was a carpenter by trade.

"But what's the message?" she asked.

I told my friend that both Annie and Anna, along with her Grandfather, would be there to help Granny make the transition when her time came. Wendy became very quiet. She knew Granny's health was failing, but the death of the woman who had raised her from girlhood was something she couldn't bear to think about. Wendy thanked me for the message and told me that she was glad to know Granny would be greeted by her family on the other side of the veil when the time came for her to join them.

Two weeks after our conversation, Wendy spoke with a medium at her own church. Without giving her any information, this spiritualist medium described both Annie and Anna to Wendy and delivered the very same message.

After giving a message from a person in Spirit, I hear almost without exception the comment that if they hadn't heard it or seen it come from me, it wouldn't have been believed. One friend in particular said, "Denise, I had no idea you were like this. I've always thought of you as an intellectual. If that had come from anyone other than you, I simply would not believe it." I received the same reaction from my sister-in-law, one evening in December of 1995.

Steve and I, along with three of his brothers and their wives, went for a holiday dinner together. Shortly after we were seated, my sister-in-law and I went to the ladies room. On the way to dinner, she and I talked about my experience with Wendy.

As we stood in the ladies room, my sister-in-law told me she always wished she had the chance to tell her grandfather how much she loved him and missed him. He passed away in 1985. She no more than said these words and I could see an older man on my 'inner screen.' I could see the letter E and asked her if this was significant to her grandfather. She told me that she believed his middle name began with an E. She then told me I was staring to give her goose bumps, so I didn't go on.

After sitting down to dinner, with my inner eye I could see a clear glass milk bottle with red letters on it. I could then see a gentleman holding the milk bottle. He was wearing navy blue work pants with a white shirt and leather belt. I apologized to my sister-in-law for bringing it up again, but I had the distinct feeling that I needed to tell her about this man. When I described the milk bottle, Joan told me her grandfather was a milkman. She then went on to confirm that she didn't remember seeing her grandfather dressed in anything other than dark blue works pants with a white shirt and belt. This is how she remembered him being dressed each day.

I then heard the words "Tell Joanie I know how she feels." I passed this message on to Joan. She told me that her grandfather did call her Joanie. When I asked her why I kept seeing an old black Royal typewriter, she told me that her grandmother had just such a machine at home. She had been a secretary for many years. Because she was very emotionally moved by this, I ended the conversation so that she could absorb what had just taken place.

One week later I saw Joan at her mother's home. She told me that her mother reconfirmed all of the facts that I had given her about her grandfather. They both expressed their amazement that I could possibly know these things, since her grandfather had crossed over long before I knew Joan and her family.

Joan then went on to tell me that since her conversation with me, she felt as though an immense weight had been lifted off her shoulders. She now felt that she knew beyond a shadow of a doubt that her grandfather knew how much she loved and missed him.

Being able to bring people together in an expression of everlasting love is a wonderful feeling. Each time it happens I feel as though I am completing a small mission from God. The next experience is perhaps the most romantic example of this, that I have experienced.

On the day after Christmas in 1996 my boss took me for our annual Christmas lunch. As we conversed during our meal, I could see a gentleman standing behind his right shoulder smoking a cigar. He continued to stand there throughout our lunch. I didn't bring this to Paul's attention until we got back to the office.

Once we were back at work, I asked Paul if he had a male relative who smoked a cigar. He replied that his father smoked cigars regularly. I described the man who had appeared during lunch as wearing glasses, a top hat and a dark overcoat. He was quite tall with a large build. Paul confirmed that his father did dress in both a top hat and a dark overcoat.

"And yes, he did wear glasses," Paul added.

I remarked how much he and Paul resembled one another. Paul agreed with me that they looked much alike.

As Paul and I continued our conversation, I heard this gentleman say, "Ask him who John is."

Paul's reply was simply, "John was my father." He then went on to say, "John was his middle name."

John began to show me an old blue vintage car with large white wall tires. Paul confirmed that his father had owned such an automobile.

Suddenly, I could see Paul's father as a teenager, dancing with Paul's mother in a high school gymnasium. They were happily twirling about the dance floor and I could hear the words "Moonlight Serenade." Knowing that their strict religious upbringing wouldn't have allowed Paul's parents to be dancing confused me. As that thought passed through my brain, I heard the words "Ask him anyway." So, I did.

I walked into Paul's office and said: "Paul, were your parents high school sweethearts? I know they were not supposed to be dancing, but I can clearly see your parents dancing in a high school gym."

"Yes, they were high school sweethearts and beautiful dance partners. As a matter of fact, it got them in quite a bit of trouble," he replied.

At that moment, I saw a lovely bouquet of red roses and heard John say, "Tell Janie I love her."

Paul had always referred to his mother as Louise, so I asked him who Janie was. Paul told me that his mother's first name was actually Jane.

"Would your father have called her Janie?" I asked.

He answered, "I was only 12 when my father died. I don't remember if he called her that or not. It's certainly possible." Paul asked me what the message meant.

"Your father is sending your mother his love with a bouquet of red roses," was my reply.

John then showed me a red bike with a basket on the front. I asked Paul if that bike belonged to him.

He said, "Yes, I used to deliver newspapers with that bike."

I heard John say, "Tell Paul that he's done a fine job with his mother and that I'm very proud of him." I delivered the message just as John asked me to.

Suddenly, I could feel the presence of yet another man. He showed me a two-tone Packard on a street curb. "Which of your relatives owned a two-tone Packard?" I asked Paul.

"My grandfather did."

I went on to ask, "Well why is it parked out on a city street?"

Paul responded: "Because he owned several city buildings and lived up above one of them. There was no driveway or garage to park it in," he continued.

"Tell Jane that Florence is fine and sends her love," were the words I heard next. I saw the name Florrie and a young girl dressed in turn of the century attire. She wore a dark blue dress that came just below the knees, along with dark stockings and a pair of buttoned boots. In her long, brown hair, she wore a beautiful bow. This young girl was Jane's childhood friend.

Meeting Nakoma

fter dismounting his steed, he stood and looked at me for a moment. His dark, soulful eyes told me everything I needed to know. Still, I questioned him.

"Who are you?" I inquired.

"My name is Nakoma. I am a Lakota Sioux," he responded.

"Are you my spiritual guide?" I asked.

He nodded in positive affirmation and then faded from my inner sight.

Two days later he reappeared to me. When I asked him how it was that I would know he was not just a figment of my imagination, he said "Ask Silvernail."

To which I quickly responded: "But Dan Silvernail will think I'm crazy. What can I say to Dan that will let him know I haven't lost my mind?"

"Ask him about Red Cloud," was Nakoma's answer.

Feeling rather foolish, yet wanting a confirmation of my experience, I called my Cherokee friend, Dan Silvernail. After telling him about my encounter with Nakoma, I asked Dan quite seriously if he thought I was losing my mind.

"Not at all, Denise" was his answer to my query. "Although I haven't experienced these things myself, I know others who have. Native Americans believe all living things have a spirit. What you've just told me does not surprise me."

"Nakoma tells me that you will know about Red Cloud and that by this, you will know he is real," I said.

"Yes, I know about Red Cloud," was Dan's reply. He then proceeded to tell me about the great Sioux Chief known as Red Cloud.

Sensing that Nakoma was still with me and wanting to tell me something, I asked him to show me what it was he wanted me to see. On my 'inner screen,' as I call it, I saw Nakoma and I riding together on his gray Appaloosa through a dense forest in the upper Midwest. We rode effortlessly and swiftly until we reached the end of the forest. There we came to a complete stop at the edge of a cliff overlooking the vast blue-green ocean.

Looking up and across this glistening body of water, I could see what I interpreted to be the Kingdom of Heaven. There, in hues of powder blue, were grand cupolas, turrets and domes, reminiscent of St. Basil's Cathedral in St. Petersburg, Russia.

Gazing upon this wondrous sight, I knew that Nakoma was going to travel with me, until I joined the others who had gone before me to this divine dwelling place.

I welcomed Nakoma into my life and thanked him for being my spiritual companion during this journey on earth.

The following week I attended a conference for administrative professionals at the Detroit Institute of Art. Following the formal meeting at this fabulous museum, we took a guided tour.

Because there were more than 80 of us in attendance, we broke up into clusters of 15 or sixteen. Each group had a docent who took us on a tour of a particular part of the museum. My group went on a tour of my personal favorite, the Gothic period.

As I stood in awe of these priceless art treasures, my attention was diverted to a room directly off to my left. Above the archway leading to this gallery was a sign that read, "Life's Journey." Peering through this arched opening, I could hardly believe my eyes. My heart began to race as I excused myself from the rest of the group. My eyes began to fill with tears as I got closer to my destination.

On the wall directly in front of me, was an oil painting by Thomas Sloan titled "Life's Journey – Youth," painted in 1839. Through the tears I beheld a sight I will never forget. Gently floating down a waterway in a gilded boat was a guardian angel, in the company of his earthly charge. Lying before them was their final destination. In shades of powder blue were the immense cupolas, grand turrets and glistening domes of the heavenly kingdom that Nakoma had shown me just days before.

My friend, Pat, came to check on me and to ask if I was feeling okay. I told her I was fine, but that I needed a few minutes alone and would then catch up with the group.

Sitting on the antique sofa in front of this work of art, I was enveloped by a sense of knowing that I was no heading on the life journey that God had intended for me. I didn't know where it was leading, but I knew I was not heading there alone.

Nor did I know, that my wish to meet Nakoma on the physical plane would soon come to fruition. But, through a beautifully orchestrated string of events, it did.

Signs come in many forms. At times they are found in a song that suddenly begins to play on the radio. For most people, certain songs evoke a specific memory. Perhaps it is a remembrance of a special person or of a fond time in years past. If you've ever been thinking of someone and 'your song' begins to play on the radio, you may wonder if by chance there is more than a coincidence taking place.

In my life, I have found occasions like this are a confirmation of an intuition or a forerunner of events yet to come. I am sure this is the case for everyone, though most prefer to think of it as just a fluke.

As a teenager, my brother, Tim, took Confirmation classes in the Catholic church. His instructor was a very special lady by the name of Katherine. One story concerning Katherine, or Kath, as her students fondly called her, involved a song by Rod Stewart entitled, "Forever Young."

Katherine's son heard this song on the radio and told his mother she ought to listen to it. He felt the words were perfectly suited for sending her young Confirmation group into the world full of faith in God's grace.

After listening to the words of the song, Katherine agreed.

During class one evening, Katherine led her group of Confirmation students into the main body of the church and asked them to stand and form a circle. As they followed her instructions, Katherine began to play "Forever Young" over the church sound system. Walking around the circle, Katherine placed her hands on top of each student's head and blessed them.

Tim was so impressed by what occurred at class, that he shared this special story with the rest of us.

Since that time in 1986, I always smile and think of Katherine when I hear "Forever Young" on the radio.

Knowing that there is no such thing as happenstance, I couldn't help but wonder what was in store for me when I heard "Forever Young" playing repeatedly on the radio in January of 1997. Not just once or twice, but nearly two or three times per week I heard this song. In 1997, "Forever Young" was something of an oldie. I knew that hearing it so often was significant.

Katherine was no longer employed at our local parish. I didn't know where she was, but I was certain that I would soon find out.

Near the end of that same month, one of my co-workers walked past my office and intuitively, I knew he could tell me who I might be able to talk to within the Catholic faith about my experiences as a clairvoyant.

After waving Mark into my office, I asked him if he knew anyone at the Catholic Diocese who was knowledgeable about spiritual gifts. Mark, a devout Catholic, asked me why I was interested in such a subject. I was very honest with him and told him I was both clairvoyant and for lack of a better term, a spiritual medium.

Mark told me that I was giving him goosebumps, but that he found the subject fascinating. He then gave the name and phone number of a woman that I had not seen in years. Lisa was now working at the Diocese and he felt sure that she could lead me in the right direction. His advice proved to be correct.

The following day, I phoned Lisa and spent the first few minutes renewing our friendship. I then proceeded to tell her exactly why I was calling. As I had heard many times before, she told me: "Denise, I know you're not a crazy person, so I would be happy to talk to Father for you. If it were anyone else telling me this, it might be questionable."

Lisa then excused herself for a moment to ask Father Lewis with whom I might speak. When she returned to the phone, she relayed his answer. "Father would like you to speak to a spiritual advisor by the name of Katherine."

"You've got to be kidding me," was my response. "I know of Katherine through my brother, Tim. She was his Confirmation instructor."

We both laughed at the seeming coincidence.

The very next morning, I phoned Katherine.

Although I had never been formally introduced to her, I had seen her dozens of times around the church and had always been struck by her beautiful smile. I could feel that smile over the phone as we discussed my brother, Tim , and the reason for my phone call.

We made an appointment for the following Monday. In the meantime, I made a copy of my personal journal and sent it to Katherine. In this way, she would know what I had been experiencing and would be ready to talk about it.

My initial meeting with Katherine was, for me, like going home. We opened our meeting with prayer and as she spoke to me, I noticed a lovely blue aura about her. When I commented on it, she told me that this aura had been noticed by others, during different times of her life. She shared the premonition she had, which told her when her father was going to cross over and the feelings she had about it when it finally came to fruition. She recalled giving the eulogy for her father and her sister had noticed the light of her aura surrounding her body as she spoke.

Katherine exuded a warmth of spirituality that told me all I needed to know about her nature and deep faith in God.

Reiterating words previously spoken by Sonia in Chicago, she said: "Denise, you are what the Catholic Church calls a sensitive. You see, feel and hear things that most other people are not aware of. Your body and senses are tuned in to vibrations going on a higher level. Although many people may have a glimpse of these things, they either shut it off, or choose to ignore them. In your case, being a sensitive person is who you are, and what you are about."

Katherine reminded me to take time out for myself, so that I might regain some of the psychic energy which leaves me during spiritual encounters.

"Denise, when did you know for sure that these spiritual phenomena were for real?" she asked. I told her the story of my cousin Rick. "And how did you know Katherine?" I asked in return. She then shared with me an incredibly beautiful story about an encounter she had with angels who appeared beside her bed one evening.

As we exchanged accounts of our spiritual experiences, I noticed an old wooden hay wagon at Katherine's left side. Behind the hay wagon was a very old wooden shed. Because I could also see a single red rose, I knew that someone was trying to send a message of love. The old wooden hay wagon and shed were the clues to who was sending the communication. When I asked Katherine if this made sense to her, it did not. I felt rather foolish for having asked. The vision remained with us however, for the duration of our meeting. I knew it was significant for someone. The question was who?

I've learned through experience that even though someone may not recognize the information or descriptions I am giving them, sooner or later it will come to light. It may dawn on them or come to pass some days later, but eventually it makes sense. Sometimes, that even includes me.

As I left Katherine's office, she hugged me as if we were old friends. My soul told me we have been friends for longer than either of us know.

"Well, aren't you glad to know I don't think you're strange, and relieved that I'm not going to throw Holy Water on you?" she laughed.

God was very good to me when He made Katherine my teacher.

That same evening, during meditation I had a sudden realization. I chuckled out loud when I understood who was sending and who was to receive that lovely red rose earlier in the day. In my dining room is a photograph of my great grandparents, lovebirds that they were, sitting on an old wooden hay wagon. Behind them stands the wooden shed. Holding the photo in my hands and gazing into their gentle faces, I said, "I love you, too."

Each day I ask all of my guides and teachers in spirit to keep me on my true soul path and to provide signs along the way that I am doing so. They are always more than willing to comply. Songs on the radio and unexpected correspondence from friends and relatives seem to be their vehicle of choice. Nothing quite so glamorous as what happened to my husband Steve one night in February of 1996.

After a particularly exhausting week, I met the weekend with a very heavy heart. "Please give me a sign that will tell me I'm on the proper path," I prayed. Since my own very cloudy aura was not going to be able to pick up on such information, it was given to Steve.

As I drifted off to sleep, Steve nudged me and asked, "Denise, what does a sparkly yellow aura mean?"

"Well, I responded, if you're talking about a person, it means that they are probably very creative and quite light hearted. Why, do you have a sparkly yellow aura tonight?" I said with a sleepy chuckle.

In a very concerned, almost frightened tone, he replied: "No. I don't, but something does. I know I'm not dreaming, but I can't believe what I just saw. This stuff never happens to me. I think it was meant for you."

"What was is that you saw?" I asked.

Still not convinced that I would believe him, Steve said "I'm not lying to you when I tell you this, you know."

"Yes, I believe you. I'm the last person to question anyone about strange occurrences."

Steve went on to tell me that as he was lying there in bed, looking up at the white ceiling, a three-dimensional circle that sparkled and pulsated with a golden light and came down toward him, nearly touching his face.

"Is that a good thing?" he asked.

"If it is as beautiful as you described, and if it felt uplifting, I would say yes, it is a positive sign, Steve," I said. "Congratulations on your first illumination experience. And thank you for being the messenger of the sign that I had asked for."

Later that same week, I began feeling the presence of a little boy. I first saw him while driving home from work one day. A darling child with dark wavy hair and big dark eyes. He was dressed in blue shorts and suspenders. I asked him his name and he replied: "My name is Michael. Tell Mommy it didn't hurt. I'm okay now."

This was my first experience with a child and I felt a little uncertain. I asked Nakoma to let me know that there was in fact a child trying to get through to me. As I asked this, I changed the radio station and Eric Clapton's tribute to his own son, "Tears in Heaven," began playing on the radio.

While driving to the office the following morning, I had an inkling to ask Paul if he knew this child. He told me that his brother, Brad, lost a little boy shortly after he was born. His name was Michael. I asked Paul if there was any reason that Michael's mother might perceive him to be in pain. He told me that Michael had been born with a severe birth defect. Since Paul was due to see his brother in Miami Springs later that week, he told me he would pass the message along.

Two weeks later, Paul and I were having a conversation about guardian angels. I began to think about his brother's little boy, Michael, again. While I was thinking of his brothers' son, I clearly heard the name Stephen. When I asked Paul who Stephen was, he said that it was Brad's grandson. "Michael would have been Stephens's uncle," Paul said. I told Paul that I had the feeling that perhaps Michael keeps a loving eye on Stephen from the other side.

"Who is guiding and keeping an eye on me then?" Paul asked.

"Your grandfather," was my reply.

I could see and hear the name Charles very clearly.

"Who is Charles?" I asked.

"He was my grandfather. My father's father," was Paul's answer.

I have found in my spiritual encounters that those souls who passed as an infant will present themselves to me as a child, perhaps a toddler. This simply tells me that they passed at an early age. I believe that when a child crosses over, they continue to progress spiritually like everyone else. I have also come to believe that it is the quality, not the quantity, of time spent here on earth that is important. Each of us has a purpose or a mission to accomplish. What one person may complete in a matter of hours or days may take another decades to complete.

Those in spirit may show themselves to me during different phases of their physical life on earth so that confirmation of these facts may be made. However, if someone I know in spirit is presenting themselves to me, I will often see them as I knew them just before they passed.

During my next meeting with Katherine, we discussed what I felt God wanted me to do with the gift of discernment that I had been given.

I told her I felt as though I was being called to help people realize their own very special connection to the Creator. The spiritual visions were coming much more frequently and with much more clarity.

"It gives people a tremendous amount of comfort to know that we never truly lose anyone we love," I explained. "Knowing that our loved ones continue on in spirit until we are reunited with them at the end of our journey on earth is very healing. Sharing this knowledge is my mission."

Katherine recommended that I read up on St. Francis of Assisi. His prayer of peace has always been my very favorite. She also suggested some reading on St. Therese of Lisieux and St. Theresa of Avila, both mystics in their own time.

That weekend, I purchased a book about the lives of the saints.

Glancing around at the rows of saintly biographies, I was intuitively drawn to a particular book. After gently taking it from the shelf and looking at its cover, the book fell open to the chapter on St. Francis of Assisi.

I chuckled to myself, "This must be the book I need to read!"

It didn't take me long to pour over the pages of "The Book of Saints." It was a wonderful read that only took me one evening to accomplish. The chapter on St. Therese of Lisieux was particularly fascinating to me because, despite the centuries between us, our lives seems to have much in common.

The following day I had a novena to St. Therese of Lisieux chain letter waiting for me when I arrived home from work. The letter from my friend requested that I say one Hail Mary and one Our Father before sending it along to four other friends. The correspondence promised that something spectacular would happen as a result of my efforts.

I wasn't prepared for what happened two nights later.

During my visit with Sonia months before, she recommended that I see a prominent holistic doctor in Chicago for a minor medical problem. Because I lived three hours away, I never followed through on her advice.

Little did I know that this distinguished doctor was planning to come to Michigan that fall. He was preparing to lend a hand to a holistic medical center that was coming to fruition.

Two days after receiving the Novena to St. Therese, I received a thank you letter in the mail.

I was being thanked for agreeing to serve on the advisory panel for the new holistic medical center. Although I had no clue as to how I became a member of the advisory panel, my intuition told me that I needed to attend an upcoming panel meeting.

I responded to the letter by agreeing to attend the first panel conference.

The meeting would convene at the very center where I regularly met with my spiritual director, Katherine.

On the day of the conference, I worked late and I was tired. As I got into my car that evening, I asked my spirit guide, Nakoma, for a sign that I was indeed doing the right thing by going to the advisory panel discussion.

Turning on my car radio, I was greeted by the song "Cherokee People." Listening to the words of the song, and singing right along, I knew full well that I was being divinely guided to attend the meeting. I began to laugh out loud and thought, "The sign couldn't be much more clear, now could it?"

Arriving at the conference center I entered the building with a middle-aged woman who reminded me of a 1960's 'flower child.' The woman headed for the staircase, while I walked toward the elevator.

Standing next to the elevator was a petite and elderly nun who looked at me and said enthusiastically, "You two must want to take a ride down!"

Quite sure that I was by myself, I was surprised at her comment. Instinctively, I turned and looked to my left. A Native American man was standing next to me, where moments before no one stood.

Entering the elevator together, I introduced myself. He told me that his name was Loren.

In the instant that I listened to him speak his name, I knew that something significant was going to take place that evening.

In a room brimming with dozens of tables and over 100 participants, Loren and I sat at a small meeting table with four other people. One of them was a massage therapist. Another was an aura healer. A Roman Catholic nun and a registered nurse rounded out the group. Through the loud chatter, each of us had taken a turn introducing ourselves and our occupations.

When it was my turn, I told those seated with me that during the day I worked at the newspaper. I followed that by mentioning that I was also a clairvoyant medium.

My table mates smiled at me. No words were spoken, yet I felt as though I had been accepted freely for who I truly was and am. The warmth in their smiles told me that they understood.

Sitting directly across from me, Loren looked my way and said: "It took a lot of courage to admit that, Denise. That's the first time you've spoken about it in a public setting, isn't it? Thank you for doing so."

As the others who were seated at our table chatted with one another, Loren asked me about my "gift". It was then that I broached the subject of Nakoma.

"Do you know what the name Nakoma means?" Loren inquired.

Rather embarrassed I replied, "No, I'm sorry, I don't."

"One day you will," was his knowing response.

"Do you know any Native American medicine men?" I asked.

With a slight smile on his lips, Loren responded by saying, "Many in my family do the work of a shaman. Why do you ask?"

"For as long as I can remember, I've wanted to meet a Native American medicine man or woman," I said. As a teenager, I spent long hours at my art table drawing charcoal images of Sitting Bull, Chief Joseph and others who were nameless to me. Their faces came to me in visions. I learned who the faces belonged to only after being given a book about the great chiefs."

I further explained that I have great reverence for Native teachings, and a thirst to learn more about their ways.

With a serious tone, Loren asked, "Is this an idea?"

I hesitated for a moment and responded with a sheepish, "Yes."

In a very stern voice, Loren replied, "When it is no longer an idea, and when you truly want to meet a shaman, your shaman will come to you."

That moment will stay forever etched in my memory. The energy in his voice and meaning of his words told me beyond a shadow of a doubt that Loren was far more than just another attendee at an advisory panel meeting.

Somewhere between fright and anticipation I asked, "Loren, have you ever had a Native American Spirit guide? Do you know of any who exist?"

Smiling from ear to ear he responded, "You could say that."

I sat there for a moment, stunned.

Throughout the rest of our conversation that evening, Loren did not look at me. He looked inside me and through me. At one point it became almost unnerving.

"Loren, I asked, what is it that you want to say to me? I know you want to say something. What is it? Please say it."

Loren replied in a very calm and soothing voice: "Denise, I don't have to say anything. You know my energy and I know yours."

During our time together at the panel meeting, Loren repeated a phrase that made me begin to think it was actually Nakoma who was sitting across from me.

Several times, Loren had said, "I only see what is in front of me, Denise."

I found the statement odd at first, but now I was coming to understand that he meant it literally. Loren was there for me. At that moment in time, nothing else existed for him. Only what he saw directly in front of him. Me.

"No, it couldn't possibly be. Or could it?" I asked myself.

I continued the conversation by asking Loren what religion he belonged to, if any.

He replied, "You could call me a fallen-away Catholic. I prefer to think of myself as a philosopher."

We began to talk about Jesus and some of the other avatars such as Siddhartha, the Buddha, and the prophet Mohammed. I told Loren how important I thought it was that people know the background and teachings of the many ascended masters. To me, they all spoke the word of God, only in a slightly different language.

"It certainly would help cure a lot if misconceptions and hatred toward those of other faiths, wouldn't it Loren?" I asked.

Loren agreed and continued on by saying he felt that the teachings of Jesus were just one layer of the total spirituality given to our world.

Looking into my eyes he said, "The word avatar will one day return to you, Denise."

He followed those words by saying, "Denise, only one of us is really here tonight."

I knew precisely what he meant, but could not fathom that it was truly taking place.

Looking directly into Loren's soulful brown eyes I said: "Loren, I don't belong here tonight. I don't belong sitting in a group of healers. This room is full of medical doctors, osteopaths, acupuncturists, massage therapists and Reiki healers."

"For heaven's sake, Loren, I work at a newspaper," I exclaimed.

Leaning forward across the table, Loren spoke to me: "Denise, why do you say that? You are a healer!

He continued on emphatically, "All illness originates from separation, Denise!"

I countered: "When you say it that way, Loren, I guess you're right. I do heal those who feel separated from their loved ones who have crossed over."

Loren simply smiled at me and replied, "Enough said."

Again, he thanked me for having the courage to tell others of my spiritual gifts. He went on to tell me something I've not since forgotten.

With a serious voice, Loren told me the following: "I've never known a gift that was not also a curse. However, how would we know what gifts were, if we didn't also have curses. It's the good and the bad. The light and the dark. It's the yin and the yang."

Following those words, I left the unfinished meeting, completely overwhelmed by what I had just experienced. Walking through the lobby of the conference center, I stopped to look at some upcoming program flyers and a variety of spiritual books. I needed a moment to regain my composure before facing the outside world once more.

Settling back into my car, I asked for a sign from God that what I had just experienced was real. I turned on the radio and was immediately greeted by Rod Stewart singing "Forever Young." Katherine, my spiritual advisor on earth, came into my thoughts.

"Life is good," I told myself.

When I returned home, my family was watching a movie about Native American Indian chiefs. If I had any doubts before, they were now gone.

Little Flower is what Nakoma calls me when he speaks to me. I've always thought of it as a lovely term of endearment.

When I was 13 and it came time to choose my Confirmation name, my mother and I argued over the name that I should take. I wanted desperately to take the name Catherine, after Catherine of Sienna. My mother insisted on Therese. We compromised on Catherine Therese.

Until Katherine had suggested that I do some reading about mystic saints, I knew very little about St. Therese of Lisieux. Two decades after being confirmed in the Catholic Church and taking her name, I was to learn that St. Therese of Lisieux was affectionately called "The Little Flower of God."

Two months later I met a Pottawatomie medicine woman, or shaman: a revered pipe carrier in her tribe. It was a great honor to spend time alone with this amazing woman.

I shared my story with her. This is what the shaman told me.

"Denise," she began, "your guide Nakoma is a very powerful spirit. The eagle feathers he wears in his hair when he comes to you in visions tells me this. When you asked Nakoma to appear to you in physical form, he granted you this miracle to prove to you that he walks the path of spirit with you. Always protecting you from harm.

"The man named Loren is a shaman in this physical world. In order for Nakoma to come to you in physical form, he needed medicine man's human body. Loren agreed to this and lent his physical form to Nakoma to carry out this task. You have been witness to a great miracle, Denise."

As this wise woman spoke to me, I remembered Nakoma's words: "Is this an idea? When it is no longer an idea, and when you truly want to meet a shaman, your shaman will come to you."

Sitting before me was my idea made manifest. No longer doubting the possibility of meeting a shaman, she came to me.

A decade has passed since meeting Nakoma and the medicine woman. In that time, I have learned that the name Nakoma means, "I do as I promise."

It seems that long before I was born into this lifetime, I promised to help heal broken hearts and wounded spirits.

And so it is that I continue to keep my promise.

I am now a member of the Raven Thunder Wolf Society, a sacred Lakota lodge. Throughout the year, the Society gathers at our ceremonial grounds in Michigan to perform the Inipi Ceremony of prayer and purification. Our spiritual work and community service projects are dedicated to the healing of Unci Maka, our Earth Mother, and in doing so, healing her inhabitants.

On an unforgettable evening in the autumn of 2006, during a traditional Inipi or Sweat Lodge Purification Ceremony, I was formally adopted into the Lakota Nation by Chief and medicine man, Wakinyan Sna Mani, "Thunder Snail Walking." During my adoption and naming ceremony, which was held late at night under a star filled sky of azure blue, I received one of the highest honors bestowed by the Lakota People.

To the beating of sacred drums and the chanting of ancestral songs being sung by members of the Thunder River Drum, an eagle plume was ceremonial tied in my hair by two of my new Lakota sisters, both wives of highly revered Sioux shaman. As they welcomed me into the tribe with a warm embrace, they repeated the spiritual name which had been given to me by Spirit during an Inipi Ceremony the night before, To Wakinyan Win, "Blue Thunder Woman."

Along with this great honor, I also knew that I was setting out upon a journey that would last for the remainder of this lifetime.

The following month found me in the Badlands of South Dakota, on Pine Ridge Reservation. Along with two of my Raven Thunder Wolf Society sisters, I was there helping to deliver a semi truck load of supplies from the Society and attending the funerals of three of my newly adoptive family members.

Despite my green eyes and fair complexion, I was wholly embraced by the People. Amidst the immense sorrow of losing a tribal elder and his two beautiful daughters to a drunken driver, joy was to be found in the eyes of the children who received new clothes, toys and school supplies from a group of complete strangers from Michigan, who gave to them without condition. All around me was a sense of tradition, community and family.

As they drove up to the blue, barn like storage facility on Pine Ridge Reservation, and upon seeing the proud and beautiful faces of the Lakota people waiting to greet them, John and Irene, the semi truck driver and his wife, who nearly 11 years prior had lost their 17 year old son to drowning, felt the pulse of life rush back into their veins for the first time since their own tragic loss.

They found new family, too.

During the four day wake, held in the Oglala School gymnasium, I participated in prayer ceremonies and the singing of traditional Lakota songs. Like the others around me, the tears ran freely down my face while the Porcupine Singers sang and the Thunder River Drum team beat their sacred songs of good-bye. Although I couldn't remember ever hearing the songs before that moment, the words in Lakota, flowed from my heart and through my lips as though I had written them myself.

Through air that was filled with wispy plumes of gray smoke, the result of burning sweet grass and sage, I listened to tribal holy men speak and watched as they performed ancestral burial rites old as time itself. Gently, reverently, they walked their people through the process of mourning an unspeakable loss and assisted the spirits of their loved ones in making their journey home to Tunkashila.

As they silently watched from alongside their own burial caskets, the three who had crossed over in that terrible accident, wanted desperately to let their wife and mother know that they had indeed reached their destination, and were safely home with Wakan Tanka, the Great Spirit.

In silent communication, I promised them that when the time was right, I would deliver their message.

Helping to prepare food in the school kitchen, gave me an opportunity to make new friends. As we cooked and served the several hundred mourners each day, we learned much about each other. Through weekly phone calls, we continue to become closer friends still.

On the final day of the wake, as we prepared to do the final goodbyes, a young boy of about nine, one of the first to greet me when I arrived on the Reservation, found me sitting in the crowd.

Taking me by the hand and smiling broadly, he spoke to me saying, "Denise, I know that you're new to all of this. Just follow me in the line and I will show you what to do now. We do this a certain way."

Leading me through the line up of 27 pall bearers, many wearing eagle feathers in their hair, most wearing t-shirts emblazoned with the logo of the American Indian Movement, my young friend taught me how to properly greet each Native American man with a hand shake of respect and final farewell.

I couldn't help but be moved by how proficient and matter of fact, such a young boy was at walking through death. His boyish eyes belied a Spirit that had seen much tragedy, a common occurrence on the reservation, in such a few short years.

Weeks earlier, as I smoked the sacred canunpa or prayer pipe, in the steam filled enclosure of our Inipi, I made a promise to help my Lakota family keep their ancient and spiritual traditions alive.

With the help of my Society Sisters, Nakoma, and our designated semi drivers, John and Irene, I will do as I promise.

"On that glad night, in secret, for no one saw me, nor did I look at anything, with no other light or guide than the one that burned in my heart."

St. John of the Cross (1542—1591), Spanish Mystic, Doctor of the Church, Founder of Discalced Carmelite Order, Author, "The Dark Night of the Soul."

Grandma's Cookies and the Dark Night of the Soul

It has been over ten years since I heard the life affirming words which were spoken to me by Sonia, "Denise, you were put on this earth as a psychic counselor to help people. Now, go out there and do what God intended for you to do!"

Countless people have crossed my path in the last decade. Following the publication of my first book, "Meditations from The Temple Within," and the subsequent book signing tour, lecturing at universities, colleges and places of worship have become an integral part of my life.

It has been my distinct pleasure to teach classes in spiritual and intuitive development throughout the Midwest and as far away as Cornwall, England. The thirst for 'spiritual remembering' as I call it, seems to be unquenchable in this age of hollow materialism. "After all," I tell my students, "I'm not telling you something your soul doesn't already know, I'm just reminding you of what you've always known."

Spirit is endless and our connection to the Divine is ever present. When we turn off the TV, iPod or computer and take the time to stop and listen to the voice of our soul, it will tell us all we truly need to know. The only thing that stops us from having the ears to hear and eyes to see, is us, and the fear of what we might hear or see. Most importantly, I remind people that it is impossible to separate ourselves from the love of mother/father God.

Of course, these ten years have brought opportunities to work with unwieldy poltergeists and the people who host them in their homes and businesses. After all, what would a psychic medium's life be without having to help usher a cranky ghost or two to the Light? Seems that even those on the other side get ornery when they are stuck in confusion.

I have worked with prosecuting attorneys to try and help find serial killers and their victims. I have conducted private reading sessions with clergy from as far away as Ireland and Russia and with grieving parents from places such as Mexico and Switzerland. Whether I am with a client from Kyoto, Japan, or Washington, DC, one thing remains constant. The human desire to know that this life does not end here and that death is but another chapter in our eternal existence is universal.

Following are letters from my clients, written for you, the reader. Their wish to share our experiences of Spirit together is both humbling and healing to my soul.

Since nothing is quite as healing to me as a warm chocolate chip cookie, just out of the oven, let us begin with Steve Berry:

Grandma's Cookies

Denise,

When I was a little kid, my favorite cookie was chocolate chip. I would visit my grandparents and my grandma would quite often make them for me, knowing that they were my favorite.

My grandparents lived in Florida and one summer they came to Michigan to stay with our family. My parents set up a room in the basement so Grandma and Grandpa would have their own living area.

My best friend Chris and I were always outside playing and one day we decided to each make a robins nest and place it in a tree to see if a robin would use it. It took a couple of days, but sure enough, much to my delight, a robin started using it and actually laid eggs in it. I was so happy that I ran to the house and told my grandma about it. She came out and was very surprised to find that sure enough, a robin was using the nest I had made!!

Many years later and several years after my grandma was laid to rest, I went to see Denise for a reading. Right away, my grandma came through and started telling Denise about my bird nest!!! Now, I hadn't told that story in many years and it brought back a flood of emotions. But for sure, it was my grandma because no one could have possibly told Denise about that.

My grandma then told Denise that she was making me chocolate chip cookies and when the reading was about done, Grandma told Denise to tell me that she loved me and was giving me a chocolate chip cookie.

When I returned home and opened the door, right in front of me sitting on the counter top was FRESHLY BAKED CHOCOLATE CHIP COOKIES!!!

And when I cleared the tears from my eyes, I noticed that there was one missing, the one that Grandma gave to me as the reading was coming to an end. I was an emotional wreck, what a VALIDATION!! I was so happy I immediately called my wife and told her about the reading and my wonderful loving Grandma and her chocolate chip cookies!!!

Denise has a wonderful talent that not only has helped me understand about true love and spiritual growth, but many, many others as well.

Many Blessings Denise!!!
Love,
Steve

A Brother's Love

It is amazing to me how the Universe orchestrates events for us in order to get us on our path when we get side-tracked or feel stuck. I first heard of Denise when I was at The Wege Center in Grand Rapids, Michigan getting a peri-menopause evaluation from a nurse-practitioner. The nurse asked me what I was doing for relaxation and I told her that I had been having Reiki done on me and that I was thinking of taking a class. She gave me Denise's website and I immediately checked it out that evening. I made an appointment with her for a reading and to talk to her about taking one of her Reiki classes.

When I showed up in Denise's driveway one snowy night in February of 2003, I sat in my car for a minute and asked that my brother Jim come in from the other side and my husband's grandparents as well.

To tell you the truth, I was a little nervous about going to a medium. I had never been to one before, and I had the usual stereotypical image in my head that someone with crystals hanging all over them and a moo-moo on was going to answer the door. Instead, Denise had on Tommy Hilfiger jeans and a cute red tee-shirt. I instantly liked her and felt I had met her somewhere before.

Our reading started out very informal as we chit-chatted about her background and Reiki. She told me that my grandmother was with me and that she had a child energy with her from when she had miscarried. I told Denise that I wasn't sure of this, but that I would ask my mother. As it turns out, when I checked with my mom, she did in fact remember my grandmother losing a child.

Denise then told me that my brother Jim was there and that he kept putting his arm around my grandmother and hugging her. Denise said, "He just won't leave your grandmother alone!" I immediately knew that she did in fact have my brother because while growing up, he would constantly hug my grandmother and was always sitting next to her with his arm around her. My brother died in his 50's and this was something he did even as an adult.

Amazingly, Denise then asked me if he was depressed and had committed suicide. I almost fell off my chair! Yes – he was very depressed and killed himself, leaving a wife and 12-year old son. Denise told me that he was showing her that his depression was over and she said that he now has the most beautiful aura around him. I was so relieved and happy that Jim came in right away because I had been thinking of him for many years, wondering if he was okay. I'll never forget his funeral and my two sisters who were talking about how he was probably burning in hell if he did not ask Jesus' forgiveness before he shot himself. I remember those words sticking to me as I got so upset with them. It just didn't make any sense to me that someone with a mental illness would be punished that way. After my reading with Denise, my brother has come to me in several different dreams and we have had magnificent conversations.

Another cool thing that happened in our reading was when my husband's grandmother came in and started talking in Italian. Denise was so funny because she looked over to her right and said (to the energy), "Excuse me, but could you please speak in English?" Then she looked again and said, "Thank you," and then continued on with the messages. His grandmother kept saying, "He's a good-a boy!" over and over again. That was what she always said when she was alive. Then his grandfather came in and started talking about the time it was so hot outside that they cooled off by placing cold root beers on their foreheads. Denise described my husband's grandfather wearing one of those white tank tee shirts, which is exactly what he used to wear. When I got home that evening, my husband confirmed the root beer story and the tee shirt.

At the end of the reading, I asked Denise if there was an Andrew with me. She asked Andrew to come forward and she started delivering amazing messages from him, one of which was a 'sign" that was for me. She could not see it at first, but kept hearing water running. Then she said it was a waterfall. I about passed out! I had been having waterfall dreams for about two weeks prior to this reading. Then for weeks afterward, I kept seeing 'waterfall" stuff everywhere.

I am so honored to have Denise as my teacher and mentor. She does her work with integrity and honesty and she comes completely from the heart. She is one of those unique individuals who can help those who are grieving achieve closure, validation and peace of mind.

Patti

Rainbows and Doves

Hi Denise,

Keep on keeping on – for the world is waking up at such a fast pace now!

Love Ya, Carol

My name is Carol O'Connor and I had never met Denise in person and lived clear across the country. Yet, when I had a reading with her, it was as if she was in the same room with me and I had known her for lifetimes.

During our reading, Denise mentioned a spirit guide called "Mia," and how she would show herself to me in the form of rainbows and doves. Denise was right! The doves were appearing to me each morning. I awoke each day to find them singing to me on my apartment deck! Then the rainbows would appear. Many of them right outside my window. This was so beautiful to see.

Six months ago, my 8 year old niece was in the car with her mother visiting my area and she borrowed her mothers cell phone to call me to say, "Auntie Carol, there is the biggest rainbow near you, look outside!" I was already outside standing in awe, looking at a rainbow that went from one end of town to the other, with every color in it as clear as could be. It was as if you could touch one and ride it to the other side.

Even right now, as I write this, there is a rainbow right outside my office window. When this happens I not only get to see the beautiful visual of a Spirit, but I also know we have friends on the other side helping us.

The reading that I had with Denise was a little over two years ago. Still, the "Rainbows and Doves" come to remind me that I am never alone.

Thank you, Denise!!!

Harold and the Yellow Butterfly

This is kind of a funny story – there are many that I could share with you, but this one is comical. The first time I came to see you for a reading, I have to admit that I was a bit skeptical – not in your abilities, but I guess in what exactly it was that I was searching for from you in my reading.

When I asked you if you saw my cat, Harold, you asked me if I taught him to say, "mama". I laughed because I used to make this sound to him – which did sort of sound like I was saying, "Ma, Ma." What really cinched it for me though, was that you told me that Harold had a gift for me. It was a yellow butterfly. I didn't think much of it, until I got home.

Prior to coming to your house for the reading, I did some shopping in downtown Rockford – being that I had never been there before. I loved all the cute little shops. We were in one particular shop that sold candles, and other knick knacks, and I had spied a beautiful sun catcher that, "I just had to have." I was actually antsy in wanting to get to your house for our reading and I had no intention of buying anything! However, I just had to have this sun catcher.

Anyway, to make a long story short, when I got home, and unpacked my purchase, the sun catcher had a yellow butterfly on it! I had not told you of this purchase and there was no way of you knowing that I had picked up this particular sun catcher. It was Harold's way of connecting with me through you! Thank you, Denise, I miss him very much and it is a comfort seeing that sun catcher every day that I know was sent to me from Harold, through you.

Love, Laura

I am a child of God.
That is enough.

Before I begin my story regarding my first reading and my first encounter with Denise, I would like to set the background.

My name is Sue. I was in my late thirties, a career woman. I was not able to have children, so my life focused on my job. After many years of putting my life and my self esteem into my career, I had recently been demoted from a management position to a position as a buyer.

In January, after being on the job for a mere two weeks, I went to Hong Kong on my first buying trip. The second week into my trip, I received a phone call in the middle of the night, from my father in law. My husband, who had joined me in Hong Kong while en route to Japan for business, answered the phone in our hotel room. It was not good news. My father had passed away suddenly, from a heart attack at the age of 67. I needed to return home immediately.

Once I returned to the States, a friend of mine gave me a book on dreams by Sylvia Browne. While staying with my mother in Florida for a few days, I wandered into a bookstore, a place of comfort for me. I found other books of interest by Sylvia and began reading them to pass the time. This was my first experience with anything metaphysical.

After a difficult spring, helping my mother sell her home and move into a condo, while working on my new job, my friend suggested we see a psychic, as she had been struggling with relationship issues. I agreed and set up the appointment with Denise.

When I walked in to Denise's home, it was calm, tranquil and angelic. Warm, inviting scents filled the air. I began the discussions with Denise not really knowing where to begin or what to say. Denise took the lead. She let me know that the angel of healing, Raphael, was with me. So too was my spirit guide, Rhiannon. Denise had no idea what I needed most was healing. She didn't know of my father's recent death.

Beginning with my mother's mother, loved ones from the other side began to come through with comforting messages for me. Denise's description of my grandmother as quite prim and proper was perfect. Then, my father arrived. He told Denise about his motorcycles and the flannel shirt I had given him over twenty years prior. Dad wore that shirt every day, whether it was summer or winter!

Dad spoke of "dogs," which I really didn't understand. We never had a dog. Oh! I forgot. I had placed his "dog tags" from the Navy in my purse, just in case they were needed in order for Denise to contact him in spirit. After telling me that he loved me, my father told me that my brothers, who had also passed, helped him through to the other side. He told me lightheartedly to tell my mother to stop "blaming him," and that he was working as best he could to help her sell the house. Their home sold within the next month. As he did on the physical plane, dad reported that my brother was "out fishing." That made me laugh.

After a few tears, we said goodbye.

I have since had the pleasure of visiting with my father in my dreams. In my heart, I know he is still with me on a daily basis.

I might add, that during our session, I asked Denise about having children. As I mentioned previously, I hadn't been able to conceive and had lost all hope that I one day would. To my surprise and delight, Denise told me that I would have two children in my life.

Recently, at the age of forty, I gave birth to a beautiful baby girl!

Thanks to Denise, to the Angels, to Spirit and to God, I have a sense of peace about my life and an understanding that whatever happens in my life, even though I may not be able to control it, is always for my highest good. I now know that neither my career, nor anything else material defines me.

I am a child of God. That is enough.

Peace, love and light…always.

Love, Sue

* * * *

As I type and re-read those beautiful accounts, I am left in awe of the incredible love that exists between us and our Maker.

Yet, as we forge our way through the many tribulations that we must endure in the course of living, it is easy to forget just how greatly we are cherished by Mother and Father God.

In my 40 plus years, I have come to know that my greatest trials have gifted me with a glimpse into a Divine love that is far greater than my human ability to describe it.

St. John of the Cross knew this only too well.

Each of you reading these pages does too.

It is universally true that the Dark Night comes in many forms.

Long ago, my spiritual director, Katherine, told me that many tests would greet me along my path.

"Those with spiritual gifts like yours are constantly tested to see how they will use them. Will you work on behalf of the light, or on behalf of the darkness? Before the attainment of additional esoteric knowledge and an expansion of your abilities, you will be met by trials, Denise."

Had I known exactly what she meant, I might have stayed in bed these past couple of years.

My spirit of adventure, however, is much greater than my desire to retreat from the world of perceived misgivings. "Leap and the net will appear!" has become my new mantra.

I write this next chapter as I recover from a left brain stroke which happened just 16 weeks ago.

* * * *

"Dana, you have a choice to make. Do you wish to stay, or would you like to come Home, now?"

The angel called me Dana; the name given to me by my birth mother. It is the name that has always resonated with my spirit. It is who I am.

In an almost melodious form, those were the words I heard spoken to me several hours after being admitted into the new stroke unit at Spectrum Health Downtown hospital. These startling words weren't being spoken by a member of my 'stroke team', they were being spoken by a member of my 'angelic team'. And I knew that the divine being who was speaking those words to me was very serious about the question I was being asked.

I had just returned to my hospital room, following the CAT scan of my brain. Except for the small fluorescent light that beamed eerily from the wall at the foot of my bed, and the colorful little lights of the monitoring equipment which was attached to me like tentacles of science, my room was void of light or sound.

Utter darkness surrounded and filled me.

The right side of my body was completely motionless. And yet, I could feel my body taking leave of my hospital bed.

"This isn't really happening," I told myself. "I'm only 42 years old, and frankly, I'm way too busy to be here in this hospital for very much longer."

Despite my own hollow reassurance, I continued to sense that I, my spirit, was leaving my physical body.

"What's happening to me?" I asked into the void.

"Dana, you must make a choice. Do you wish to stay on the earth plane, or do you wish to come Home now?" a voice answered in the dark.

"Who is speaking to me?" I asked.

"Michael," was the reply.

"I can't leave yet, Michael. I promised Dane and Elyse that I would be coming home to them," I explained. "Before Darlene and I left for the hospital, Dane asked me if I was coming home. Despite my attempt at calming his fears, my son asked me what would happen to him and Elyse if I didn't live through this," I continued.

"Mom, people die from strokes," were Dane's tearful last words to me.

"I have to stay here on the physical plane, Michael," I explained. "I made a promise that I would be coming home to my kids when this is all over."

In a reassuring voice Michael responded, "It's not over yet, Dana, but when it is, have faith that everything will be alright."

As I let those words and the experience of the previous few minutes replay in my mind, I could feel myself coming back fully into my body.

Breathing a sigh of gratitude and relief, I watched from my hospital bed as a tall, slender, male nurse with light brown hair entered my room.

"Hi Denise. My name is Michael," he began. "I'm the nurse who will be taking care of you until morning."

I smiled inside of myself, as I responded from a mouth that was now flaccid on one side, "Thank you, Michael, it's been a very long day."

"By the way, Denise, what did you do to Carol?" Michael asked. "She gave her two week notice shortly after she checked you into your room?"

"It's a funny thing that happened, Michael. Well, cosmically funny, I guess. I'm quite certain Carol's not laughing," I said.

My hospital stay began like this:

Having been kept in the emergency room for nearly 5 hours as doctors worked diligently to try nd find out the cause of my stroke, a room was finally made available at around 10 p.m. in the brand new Stroke Unit. Opened just a few weeks prior, it was the jewel of the hospital.

As she had been for all of those five hours, my dear friend, Darlene, was still at my side as the hospital clerk wheeled me into my state-of-the-art private room. The very helpful and pleasant young man who escorted me to my room, was suddenly replaced by a person I promptly named "Nurse Ratchet."

"How long have you been here?" she demanded.

"About five hours, I believe," was my response.

"No, she continued on angrily, I don't mean how long have you been here at the hospital. How long have you been in this room?"

"Maybe five or ten minutes at the most," I said.

"Well, no one told me you were coming. I am not prepared for your arrival," she snapped.

Hoping to alleviate some of her obvious anger, I responded "Well, surprise, I'm here."

"I'll be back in a minute," was all she could muster.

As Nurse Ratchet left the room, I told Darlene it was okay for her to go home. I could tell that she wasn't at all comfortable with leaving me alone, especially with the specter of my having to spend the next while with my less than affable nurse. After some more coaxing, she finally acquiesced and returned home to her family.

Shortly after Darlene left, a very huffy Nurse Ratchet again entered the room. She promptly placed a stack of papers on a clip board and a pen on my lap.

"Here. Fill these out and I'll return to get them shortly," she ordered.

As her dutiful new charge, I did as I was told. However, while my brain knew exactly how to do what she has asked me to do, my right hand and fingers simply couldn't. My attempt at picking up the pen, landed it on the floor near my hospital bed. The clipboard and papers were soon to follow as I attempted to reach the fallen pen.

Now beginning to understand the magnitude of what was happening to me, I became both frightened and frustrated.

"Don't do this to me!" I shouted out loud to no one in particular. "This can't happen now," I pleaded.

And then the tears of frustration and anger came. They came in uncontrollable waves, one right after the other. Like the right side of my body, I had no control over the burning tears that now ran down my face and onto my hospital gown.

Nurse Ratchet must have heard my anguish from outside my hospital room. Slowly and silently she entered my darkened room, picked the clipboard up and pen from the tiled floor and retreated from my dimly lit room.

What happened next is a scene I shall never forget.

Entering my hospital room one last time, Nurse Ratchet leaned over the metal rails of my hospital bed and very calmly and with great compassion said, "Denise, I don't know why I am about to say what I'm going to say. I just know that I'm going to say it."

With a look of reticence upon her face she continued, "Denise, your mind does not know the difference between reality and fantasy. If you see your body as whole and healthy, that is what it will become."

As if in a trance that had suddenly been broken, she apologized profusely to me for her unsolicited comment. "I hope I haven't offended you, Denise. I'm not quite sure where that came from, but I felt compelled to say those things. Please forgive me if I've upset you."

In that moment of compassion, Nurse Ratchet became Carol to me.

I responded to her timely communication with, "Thank you, Carol, for delivering that message. It's something that I teach others, but right now, in this moment, I had forgotten about it. Thank you for being the messenger of that much needed reminder."

Carol smiled briefly, almost embarrassed and said, "You're welcome, Denise."

Once again, she took my vital signs. That was the last time I saw Carol. While I was being whisked away to have a CAT scan done of my brain, she gave her two week notice of resignation.

Now, I was talking to my new nurse for the night, Michael.

From within myself, I heard the angel's voice say to me once again, "It's not over yet, Dana. It will be over with very soon All is well."

From outside myself, I heard, "It's time for your MRI, Denise. Are you ready?" It was Michael my new male nurse.

"Ready as I'll ever be," I slurred.

Michael smiled and helped me into the cold wheelchair which would carry me down to the MRI staff. After covering me with warm blue blankets, we began our journey down the maze of hallways together.

Two female technicians greeted me upon entry into the sterile MRI scanning room. One was wearing a clinical smock covered in colorful images of flying angels. The other wore a gold angel pin on her smock's lapel.

"We've been expecting you," they seemed to say almost simultaneously.

I thought to myself, "I'm certain you have. And I'm very certain that we are not alone in this room right now." I could feel the presence of my Aunt Mary Lou.

With a smile in her voice, I heard auntie say, "You're going to be okay, DaNiece." I didn't know whether to laugh or cry, so I did both as I prepared to enter the MRI chamber.

In the next moment, the technician sporting the angel pin asked if she could hold my necklace for me, along with the gold ring on my left thumb. I was wearing my aunt Mary Lou's thin gold wedding band. The dainty gold ring hadn't left my hand since the day she made her way back Home in 1993. It had become my way of keeping her with me, despite the distance that 'the veil' placed between us.

"That's a beautiful gold medallion on your necklace, Denise. Is that the Holy Mother?" the technician inquired.

"No, it's Mary Magdalene. I've been very fond of her since I was a young girl," I explained.

As I spoke, I tried to remove my own necklace. It proved to be more of a challenge than I could overcome.

"I'm afraid you're going to have to take my necklace off for me," I told the tech. "My right side has decided to take leave for the moment, and my left side is rather confused by it all."

"I'll take good care of her for you while you're in the MRI tube, Denise," she said with a smile. "Everything is going to be okay."

Slowly, I entered the silver, metal tube. With the top of the tube only inches from my nose, I closed my eyes and listened to the muted and rhythmic jack hammering sound of the MRI machine. The steady cadence put me into a deep, meditative state.

"Dana, it's still not over, but soon will be." It was the archangel Michael again.

"What do you mean by 'over'?" I inquired telepathically. "Does that mean the next stop is the Pearlie Gates? I thought we had agreed that I was going to stay here on the earth plane."

In a deep and soothing voice he reassured me, "Yes, Dana. You have chosen to stay and continue your work; and it is so. However, your physical body is not done processing this illness. Remember, all is well and as it should be."

Following this angelic conversation, I was given visions of what was in store for me now that I had chosen to remain on earth. I look forward to the time when I am able to share those visions as things that have come to fruition. Life experiences that are both glorious and painful.

For now it was time to return to my hospital room and to the comfort of the dark silence that awaited me there. My nurse, Michael, tucked me safely back inside the crisp white sheets and comforting blankets of my hospital bed, and gently shut the heavy wooden door to my room.

It was then, in the wee hours of the morning, that I heard what I had been waiting to hear for over nine hours.

"Dana, it is now over. Your healing has begun." Those were the last words the angel Michael spoke to me.

After 24 hours in the hospital I was unable to walk on my own, or write my own name. I kept thinking about the previous night and Michael's words to me. I thought also about the divinely inspired words of Carol, a.k.a. Nurse Ratchet: "Remember Denise, your mind does not know the difference between reality and fantasy. If you see your body as whole and healthy, that is what it will become."

The team of orthodox doctors inside the hospital and the teams of energy healers outside the hospital began their work in earnest. The prayer circles on my behalf had begun and miracles started to manifest daily.

When the specialists and therapists made comments about the laughter coming from my room, I understood it came from a place of curiosity. After all, how could a 42 year old woman who had suffered a stroke find joy and laughter in the situation? I couldn't walk on my own. I couldn't even put the round pegs in the round holes and the square pegs into the square holes without great effort. But I was still laughing. My face was lopsided and my speech slow, but I was smiling. Why?

I knew the answer to those questions. I had known since my first day upon this earth. I knew that I wasn't alone and that everything, absolutely everything, happens for a reason and that after every storm comes the rainbow. The rainbow wasn't anywhere in sight at that moment, but I knew it would be coming. At first it came in the form of prayers from friends, family, clients and students. It came in the form of healing intentions from energy healers all over the world.

And the doctors could feel it. They couldn't explain it, but they could feel it.

The physician who put it most succinctly was the team psychiatrist who was called in on the last day. My team was concerned that I might need an antidepressant to help me cope with the changes that a stroke and a divorce had brought to my life. They also felt that perhaps it might help with the emotional and physical strain that would take place during the coming months of physical and occupational therapy.

I would have none of it.

They didn't understand.

Because of my attitude, the team psychiatrist was called in to speak to me. To put some sense in my head, or so they thought.

My meeting with Dr. Urban began with this question: "Denise, there's more going on here than meets the physical eye, isn't there?" She continued, "I mean, more than just a left brain stroke. From what you've told your doctors, you feel this is part of your spiritual journey. A test of faith, if you will."

"The dark night of the soul comes in many forms, doctor. Sometimes it even comes in the form of a stroke. But, with every dark night comes a new dawn. I'm facing a new dawn as a single woman, a single mom, and as a soul who has chosen to continue to walk a mystic's path," I explained.

"Didn't you tell the doctors that you knew you were having a stroke because you lost the sight in your right eye?" she asked.

"Yes, I did," I said nodding my head.

"I knew when I was called in to see you this morning, that this wasn't going to be my typical meeting," the doctor continued. " I just had a feeling. As I was walked out of my house, I took a long look at my favorite painting of all time. "The Conversion of St. Paul," by Caravaggio. I have it hanging on my living room wall. As I was gazing at the picture of the Apostle Paul being blinded by the Light of Heaven, these words came into my mind, "I once was blind, and now I see.""

With a knowing smile she asked, "This stroke happened to help you see, didn't it Denise?"

Returning her warm smile, I replied, "Yes, doctor, it did."

For the next several minutes, Dr. Urban and I talked about the way in which I was going to walk through the fire that life had brought me in the form of a major illness.

"I can mask my reality with drugs, or I can look it straight in the eyes and confront it, doctor. Blame it on the Army brat in me, or call me crazy, but I plan to deal with it face to face," I explained. "I know it's going to be ugly at times, but no one ever said that being forged by the fires was fun."

We shook hands as she left my room. Smiling, she said, "It's been a pleasure speaking with you today, Denise. I hope we have the chance to talk again, one day."

As the last physician to see me during my four day stay at the hospital, Dr. Urban reported her findings to the rest of my stroke team that afternoon. Later that day, after much discussion and hand wringing, the leader of my team of physicians entered my hospital room.

"Denise, while all of us on your medical team are delighted with your progress following this episode, we are still puzzled as to how this happened in the first place," he began. "Your scans are clear, your internal organs are perfectly healthy, and yet it's obvious that something major has happened, resulting in the limited use of your right side," he went on.

"The way in which this stroke began, isn't clear. What is clear however, is that we are not able to do anything further for you here in the hospital. You've talked to us about the power of the prayers you're receiving and how they've helped you heal. You told us about visualizing yourself as whole and healthy and about the morning meditation to facilitate that. And, you've told us about your friends and students who continue to send energy healing intentions to you."

"We have no other way of explaining your rapid progress. Four days ago, you couldn't even stand by yourself. You're now walking with a cane. You couldn't write your name and now, albeit with great effort, you can. We're beginning to believe that the prayers and visualization and healing intentions really have made a huge difference for you," he said, slowly shaking his head.

"With that in mind, we are going to let you go home to fully recover. As much as we would like to keep you here until we get to the bottom of this, we know there is nothing here for you. What you need is out there, waiting for you," he said with a smile.

With a gentle handshake he said, "You've been a pleasure, Denise. I wish you well."

"Thank you doctor, I responded, everything in life happens for a reason. This did too."

"Somehow I knew you were going to say that," he chuckled.

While there is great laughter to be found in these humbling life experiences, my son, Dane has been relieved of having to tie his mother's shoes, and my daughter Elyse no longer has to help me fix my hair. Darlene is no longer my babysitter, taxi driver or co-grocery shopper. Mary Ann is no longer the head cook on duty, trying to figure out what two teenagers might like to eat for dinner each night.

With every new day comes further healing of my body and spirit. The dawn is beginning to show itself after such a long, dark night.

My ability to 'see' has grown immensely.

My spiritual director was ever so correct in telling me that along the mystic journey, my faith and spiritual integrity would be tested. The end of my 20 year marriage and the subsequent stroke tested my spiritual mettle like nothing before.

"To everything there is a season, and a time to every purpose, under heaven." I tell myself this each day. Even when the day is spent looking for a young man gone missing.

* * * *

"How far is heaven?" I began hearing those words being sung by Los Lonely Boys on the radio days before I received my first phone call from a woman asking me to help locate a young man who disappeared from a gathering only days earlier.

While speaking to this woman, I could clearly see a young man with dark hair and lovely dark eyes. He was lying on his back, completely submerged beneath about a foot of water and a thicket of dark green lily pads.

"He's in the water. More specifically, he's stuck in the mud and lily pads." Those were the first words I uttered in response to her request for help.

"Really?" she replied. "His last phone call to a friend indicated that he was lost in a field near the place he was last seen."

"That may be where he last phoned from, but that's not where you'll find him," I assured her.

"Would you be willing to drive up north and help us look for him?" she asked.

"Of course, I answered, where shall we meet?"

After taking the directions down on paper, I phoned my friend Darlene and asked her if she would like to go with me to help find this man. Always ready for an adventure, she agreed to go with me. A short time later we met at my house and began the half hour drive up north to begin the search for Allen.

Just as Christy described it, her bright red pickup truck greeted us at our designated meeting place, a savings and loan building several miles south of where Allen was last seen.

Following personal introductions, we climbed back into our respective vehicles and I followed Christy to the exact spot where Allen was known to have been. It was an area of mature fruit trees and dense woods.

Pointing in the direction of a bonfire pit full of ashes, beer cans and whiskey bottles, Christy began to tell me about Allen's disappearance. "This is the spot where Allen's friends last saw him," Christy began.

"Christy, I know you're just trying to help me, but please don't tell me anything more about this spot or about Allen. I need to focus on what my senses are telling me and any information you might give me may cloud my perceptions," I explained.

"Okay, I understand," she replied. "I'll just let you do your thing."

My intuition led me directly north of the site. I found myself standing on a ridge, looking down through a thick stand of trees and knee high weeds.

Speaking to no one in particular, I stated, "He's went down here."

"But he wouldn't have gone that way," was Christy's response. "His home is in the opposite direction."

Unmoved by her statement, I bent down and stepped through the wires of an old electric fence. With Darlene directly behind me, we made our way down a rugged hill, with no clearly defined path.

Clutching onto branches in an attempt to keep our footing, I could sense Allen's desperation. He wanted to be found. It was his beckoning call that pulled me down the hill and through the dense trees.

"He's down here, Darlene," I said. "I can feel him. He's in the water. We're going to find a small wooden structure of some sort. He'll be near that place," I continued.

Reaching the bottom of the hill, we were greeted by a search team and a blood hound named Grace.

"Who are you?" they asked.

"I'm here to help in any way I can," was my answer.

"Okay, well just stay out of Grace's way or she won't be able to pick up on Allen's scent," was the reply.

"I'll stay as far away as I can," I assured them.

"The reason she's not picking up on Allen's scent, I told Darlene, is because he is in the water, not on the ground. With all the rain we've had these past several days, his scent is long gone."

"I think you're right, Denise." was all she could say as we both locked our gaze upon a small lake before us and a wooden hunting blind just beside us.

Very quietly I asked, "Can you feel him, Darlene?"

"Yes, she said, slowly nodding her head in agreement, I can."

"He's right here in front of us. I'm sure of it Darlene."

Before we could move any further ahead, Grace began to yelp in that soulful way in which only bloodhounds do. She hadn't located Allen, but she did manage to find Darlene and me staring at the lake full of tall grass and lily pads.

A member of the search team looked up at us and said, "We're sorry ladies, but we're going to have to ask you to leave the area. You're confusing Grace."

"Have you checked the area just around the rim of this small lake?" I asked.

In a very confident and somewhat perturbed manner, he replied, "Yes, of course we have. There's nothing there. Grace hasn't picked up any leads during our search of this entire area."

As we turned around to head back, I looked at Darlene I said, "We'll come back here later, when Grace is no longer here. In the meantime, let's climb back up that hill and talk to Christy about our impressions."

The steep ascent to the top of the hill was made even more grueling by the intense humidity and hot summer sun beating down on us. Despite that, we weren't willing to throw in the towel just yet. Allen was waiting to be found.

"Christy," I called to get her attention, we're back."

"You weren't gone very long." she said with a puzzled look. "I thought you'd be down there a lot longer than that."

"There is a tracking team down at the bottom of the hill and we were getting in the way of things," I explained.

As I was explaining my psychic impressions and telling her that I believed Allen was in the small lake at the foot of the hill, I could hear Allen talking to me in an urgent and pleading manner.

"Denise, please tell her that it was an accident. No one hurt me on purpose. Yes, there was a scuffle, but it had nothing to do with any of this. It was all an accident. I was drunk. Going home I got disoriented, and I walked straight into the water. The mud and muck sucked me into the lake up to my knees. The harder I tried to get out, the worse it got. I drowned! Please tell her to tell my family, this is all a horrible accident!"

Once again I could see the handsome face of this young man submerged in the waters His body was being held firmly in place by the tall grass, mud and lily pads.

Thinking out loud, I answered him, "I'll tell her exactly what you've told me, Allen." And so I did.

Christy listened intently as I relayed Allen's message. She was obviously confused by what I was telling her. No one saw him walking toward the lake. In fact, no one recalls seeing him leave at all. One minute he was at the party and next he was just gone.

"I just don't understand it Denise, Christy began. Allen lived in the opposite direction. He called his friend after midnight and told her he was lost in a field. From the sound of his voice she knew he had been drinking too much. Christy continued, Allen sounded as though he was out of breath, like he'd been running or something. Before Katie could ask him anything more about where he was, his phone went dead."

At that moment, I heard Allen say, "I'll show you where I lived, Denise. I just moved there not too long ago. Follow me and I'll show you. My dog is there. He's been acting up ever since I died. He knows I'm over here."

I looked at Darlene and Christy and repeated what I had just heard. "Allen says he just moved here recently and that his dog has been acting up since he disappeared four days ago. He wants me to follow him and he'll show me where he lived."

Christy phoned her boyfriend to confirm this information. As she hung up the phone a big smile came across her face as she told me "You're right, he did just move here and yes, his dog is still at home with his roommates."

"Okay, Denise. Let's go. I know where Allen lived, but I'll follow your lead." was Christy's response.

"This way," I heard Allen say.

Following the direction of his voice I turned to find him standing in front of me, wearing denim jeans, a black t-shirt, work boots and a baseball type cap on his head.

Through the trees and out to the dirt road we went.

I could hear Christy talking to Darlene just behind me. "This is really strange, Darlene. I've never done anything like this before. You know, working with a psychic. I've seen this kind of stuff on TV but I've never experienced it in person."

"How do you know Allen?" Darlene asked.

"I really didn't know him very well, she answered. In fact, I don't know his family at all. My boys knew him, though. Ever since Allen disappeared, all I can think about is my own sons. If it were either one of them, I would hope that people would help me in any way they could. I guess you could say I'm doing this as a concerned mother."

Darlene replied, "That's really nice of you, Christy. I have no doubt that one day, if you ever need help, people will be there for you, too."

Arriving at the end of the dirt road we were confronted by a busy highway. As we stood at this intersection, Allen said, "Follow me over the road, Denise. I lived down on the other side of that hill by the lake. I always walked the railroad tracks to get back home. You'll see."

Informing Christy and Darlene as to what I had just been told I said, "We need to cross the highway, ladies. Just over the hill are railroad tracks. That's the way Allen used to go home after the bonfires."

True to his word, Allen led us over the road, down a steep hill and to a set of railroad tracks that wound along side a small lake.

With a nod, Christy confirmed the information I had just been given. "Yep, this is where he lived alright. If we follow the tracks they'll take us directly behind his home here on the lake."

Allen was now walking in front of us and singing "Over the river and through the woods to Grandmothers house we go!"

Two weeks later, I would learn that Allen referred to his aunt and uncle who lived near him on the lake, as Grandma and Grandpa. They too lived along the railroad tracks that took us past the modest white house that Allen shared with his cousins and his dog, Brutus. It was Allen's uncle who confirmed this term of endearment with Christy, after hearing her describe Allen singing this classic American tune.

Despite our efforts in trying to turn the focus of the investigation from the open fields and barns to the small lake I felt sure Allen was calling to me; professional investigators and volunteers alike continued to scour the surrounding orchards and corn fields for any sign of Allen.

Knowing that we would have to take a different tact in finding him, I asked Allen to describe for me what he was experiencing.

"Denise, I am stuck in the lily pads and muck. I can't get out of here, please help me. I'm trapped inside this body and in this lake!" Allen continued his plea for help with "Please do something to help me, Denise!"

At that moment, I rejoined the group of women, now joined by Christy's sister, Jane, and asked them to gather around in a circle with me.

"Ladies, I began, we are going to take time right now to help Allen in a different, yet equally important way. He tells me that he is trapped within his physical body and within the muck and mire of the lake. Perhaps if we can help his spiritual body to leave his physical body, it will help lighten him enough so that his physical body will naturally surface to the top."

Glancing at one another and nodding in agreement, my companions silently formed a small circle.

"How are we going to make this happen?" asked Jane

"By calling on Allen's angels and loved ones on the other side to help us," I responded.

"Was Allen a Christian?" I asked.

"I believe his family goes to church," was the answer I received from Christy.

"Well then, I said, we will begin by asking Jesus to help Allen, come home to Heaven. Apparently, his confusion and anger is keeping Allen from doing this himself. Since he has asked us to help him, we'll ask on his behalf."

Holding hands, I began to speak for the group, "Heavenly Mother, Divine Father, we ask you for help this day. On behalf of Allen, we ask Jesus, the Angels of Heaven and Allen's loved ones to come to the aid of his spirit, which is being held within his physical being, rendering him unable to come back Home to You. Please welcome Allen home into the loving radiance of the Creator, and help his physical body to surface, so that his loved ones on Earth can put his physical body to rest."

After making a request for divine intervention on behalf of the group gathered, I asked each one of them if they would like to contribute anything further. As each one of the women expressed their gratitude for the help that would be coming to Allen, all of us could feel the energy in the air begin to lift. Internally, I could see Allen taking the hand of a magnificent angel who lifted his spirit up through his body, the dark sediment, the lily pads and ultimately through the surface of the murky water in the lake.

I announced excitedly, "It's happening ladies! Allen is leaving his physical being and going home! They'll find his body very soon now, and everyone will be able to rest, including Allen."

Feeling a sense of optimism and accomplishment, we hugged one another and went our separate ways.

A day later, while driving home from the West Michigan lakeshore, I received a phone call from my son, Dane.

"Mom, you were right!" Dane continued, "They found Allen exactly where you said they would! The man who owns the private lake found him floating on top of the lily pads this morning! You were right all along!"

I thanked Dane for letting me know that Allen's physical body had been recovered, and I thanked Mother Father God for answering our plea for help so quickly.

In the moment that I expressed my gratitude, I could hear Allen say, "Thank you, Denise. Please thank everyone who prayed for me, too. I didn't even know any of you personally, but you helped me anyway. Thank you. Please let everyone know I am okay now."

Six months later, the group of us, with the exception of Jane met for dinner. After starting my car and heading down the road to meet my new friends, a very special song came on the radio. "How Far is Heaven", began to play. It made me chuckle to know that Allen was keeping tabs on us, and would be there to help us celebrate our new friendship.

My life continues to lead me down winding paths to new adventures and new friendships. What I have learned as I walk my path, is that all of us have a story to tell. All of us have a mystic that lies deep inside, sometimes dormant for many years or even an entire lifetime. At some point during our earthly journey, the voice of the Divine that resides within us, wishes to come forward and to speak. Our soul longs to connect with Spirit in ancient ways that have long been forgotten by many.

The voice of our Soul speaks to us daily. If we choose to 'listen' with our hearts, our eyes, and our ears, we find that truly, we are never alone. All knowledge from all time is within us. With patience and practice, each one of us, regardless of race, creed, or gender has the ability to engage fully with Spirit.

The second half of this book is about just that. Learning to 'listen' and to respond to the voice of our spirit, or what some have come to call our higher self; that part of us that still walks fully in the grace of the divine as our physical body walks an earthly existence.

What is presented in the coming chapters are ways in which you too, can access the ageless wisdom of your soul. I have been teaching these simple exercises for over a decade to people from all walks of life from around the world. Whether I am teaching a medical doctor, who wishes to gain insight into the spiritual workings of his/her patients, or a college student who is trying to find out 'what it's all about,' I take great delight in watching the mystic within each of them emerge from the chrysalis that has housed their spirit on the physical plane.

With a spirit of joy and a light heart, I ask you to step into your inner wisdom, as you come to know your own unique mystic within.

*"Mystical science is a chalice of golden wine...a new song
for the hearts of the children of the new age."*

Emma Curtis Hopkins, (1853-1925) author of "High Mysticism",
founder of the Emma Hopkins College of Metaphysical Science

Part Two
A Guide to Meeting
The Mystic Within

"There are two mistakes one can make along the road to truth
... not going all the way, and not starting."

Buddha, Orig. Siddhartha Gautama, (563?—483? b.c.e.)
Indian mystic and founder of Buddhism

Dedication

Part Two of this book is dedicated to my two mystics in the
making, Dane Andrew and Elyse Marie-LaFave; that they might
walk their own Mystic Journey with Light Feet and a Joyful Heart.

Introduction

Walking the Mystic Journey is a way of living in tune with our connection to the Divine. Just as gardeners tend to their precious flowers, we too must tend to our Spiritual Garden. By helping our soul blossom, we become a wondrous manifestation of Heavenly Light on this earthly plane.

Journeying along the path of Spirit is no easy task. Yet, as we make our way through life, experiencing our Selves as a part of the greater whole, we are blessed by the realization that we do not walk the path alone. We are always in the company of our Guides, Angels and Teachers in Spirit. Like the Gardener who cultivates new growth from the tilled earth, we are called to nurture our own growth from the soil we have tilled from within our Soul.

Traveling in the Realm of Spirit takes practice. We must hone our Spiritual Gifts, like an athlete training for Olympic competition. The more we practice, the more 'spiritually fit' we become. It is important to take time each and every day to train our Psychic Selves through meditation, exercise, proper eating and positive thinking. We must maintain balance in our bodies and in our lives.

The Mystic Journey is not a boastful path, but a quiet way of living in sync with Spirit. It's about having the courage to go within and retrieve the Light that each of us carries. Once this Light has been retrieved, it will illuminate a way of living in this world, fully connected to our true Home and to our Heavenly family.

As you interact with this workbook, you will be asked to consider your own Mystic Journey and the experiences you have had until this point. You will be asked to expand your way of being in this world, but not of this world. Most importantly, you will be encouraged to embrace your divinity and to let go of ideas and things that no longer serve the journey of your soul. In this way, we shall clear a path for the many exciting adventures that lie ahead.

With that in mind, let the Mystic Journey continue...

Rules of the Mystic Journey

While walking the Mystic Journey, it is important to be mindful of a few rules of the road. As with any aspect of your life, boundaries and proper decorum help keep your path focused and filled with integrity.

Following are the rules of the journey as I practice them. Please feel free to add your own thoughts and ideas:

- Remember that Knowledge is power and you are held responsible for how you use your Knowledge and thus, your power.
- Do not assume that everyone is ready for psychic guidance. Never give psychic guidance unless it is asked for.
- Psychic guidance is about empowering others so that they might live their lives fully.
- Psychic guidance is never demanding or pushy. Go gently and compassionately, realizing that not everyone is in the same spiritual 'place.'
- Trust in the Universe and *know* that you are being guided by Divine Grace.
- Remember that every encounter is a Holy Encounter.
- There is no 'good' or 'evil' only high vibration energy and low vibration energy.
- Like attracts like.
- What goes around, comes around to teach us how to look in the mirror.
- Light always shatters the Darkness. Love always wins.
- Treat yourself and your body with the same respect you would show another.
- You can become bogged down and serious as you walk the Mystic Journey, or you can laugh and play along the way. It's your choice. Choose to have fun!

What does the word "mysticism" mean?

Of or relating to immediate consciousness of the transcendent, or ultimate reality, of God. The experience of mystical communion. A belief in the existence of essential realities beyond perceptual or intellectual apprehension.

Do all world religions have mystics? Absolutely. We need only to look at the likes of Confucius, Black Elk, Abraham, Mohammed, Gibran, and Rumi to realize that mystics have lived throughout the world, throughout various religions throughout all time. These individuals were able to transcend the physical and fully realize and commune with the spiritual. The legacies that they leave us are treasures beyond measure.

We, too, are called to be mystic: to realize the infinite potential within us and to access the infinite wisdom that resides in our connection to the Divine. By traversing your Temple Within, you are walking upon sacred ground, which will lead you to who you truly are; a spark of the Divine, a child of the Creator, a part of All That Is. It is in remembering who we truly are that we are able to hear the voice of our Higher Self and tap into a realm long forgotten by our physical selves.

What does the word "psychic" mean?

It simply means, "of the soul."

Therefore, psychic guidance is the guidance of the soul.

Since we are all souls, we are all psychics!

We are all a spark of the Oneness, the Divine. And as such, we remain forever connected to the Source of All That Is. We are part of it, and it is part of us. By accessing your psychic self, you are accessing that part of you which is fully connected to the Source, God, Goddess, and the Creator.

Once you have put the Universe on notice that you intend to use your psychic or soul gifts, you must expect that psychic or soul guidance is coming your way. We are always being guided by the still, small voice from within. The difference between the ordinary person and the mystic is that the mystic looks beyond the mundane to 'see' and 'hear' the guidance that is being given. The mystic realizes that we are always in the company of God's messengers and that we are eternally connected to the source of the Creator's wisdom. As you begin the Mystic Journey, know that you are fully supported along the path. You must simply "open your eyes, your ears, and your heart" in order to receive the guidance that is available to you.

"There is no reality except the one contained within us. That is why so many people live such an unreal life. They take the images outside themselves for reality and never allow the world within to assert itself."

Hermann Hesse (1877-1962), German-born Swiss writer, 1946 Nobel Prize winner for literature

Divine Guidance and Our Cosmic Antenna

hink of your aura or chakra energy system as an antenna that receives universal information or communications from Spirit. It works much like a radio or television in that it receives what is perceived to be invisible electronic transmissions that are then converted into feelings, sounds and visions. We receive this information through our psychic or intuitive faculties:

Intuition - The still, small voice from within. Also known as "women's intuition" or "gut feeling." Intuition is the voice of your Soul and of your Higher Self. Your Higher

self is that part of you that resides in the realm of the Divine.

Intuition is that feeling that tells you to pick up the phone and call your friend. And in doing so, finding out that your friend has been thinking of you and wishing you would call. It is also that voice from within that tells you to take another route to work, only to find out later that there had been a terrible accident along your ordinary route.

The "Clairs"

The Clairs, as I call them, are the means by which our physical and our etheric bodies receive psychic or soul information. Because each of us is different, each of us receives psychic guidance in a slightly different manner.

While some people receive this information through all of their clairs, others may have one or two clairs that are more highly attuned than others. This doesn't mean that we can't work on opening all of our clairs to receive divine guidance. Of course we can!

Clairvoyance

Clairvoyance means, "clear vision." This is the seat of our third eye, which is located just above the brow in the center of our forehead. Intuitive or psychic information that is received through this energy center comes in the form of visions or of being able to see beyond the physical realm and into the realm of Spirit.

When I work as a psychic medium, I am using my third eye to see Angels, Spirit Guides or people who have crossed over into Spirit.

Just as I see with my physical eye, my spiritual eye also sees very clearly those in Spirit. Many times when a person who has crossed over, 'steps through', as I call it, into my view, they will show themselves to me as they looked just before they crossed over. In the case of very young children who have passed on, they will appear to me first at the age at which they crossed over. Some will then show me what they now look like, having matured on the other side, just as they would have here.

In some cases, loved ones will wear something that they were particularly fond of wearing in their physical incarnation.

One such young man, by the name of Sam, presented himself wearing Tommy Hilfiger denim jeans, white sneakers and his most prized possession, a black leather coat.

Upon giving his parents this description of their smiling son, they looked at each other and began to laugh, knowing just how fond their son was of his Tommy Jeans, white tennis shoes and his favorite thing of all, his black leather jacket.

This gave his parents an instant recognition of their son and of the fact that he was happy, healthy and very much alive on the other side.

In yet another example of how clothing tells a story, I once read for an elderly woman from Poland who had survived the second world war, but who at a young age, had been forced to flee from her home in order to escape the wrath of the invading German army.

As I read for Viola, a woman who told me her name was Margaret, appeared standing alongside her. Margaret was wearing WWII era clothing, but with a yellow Star of David on her sleeve. She then began to show me a 'movie' on my inner screen about how she met my client, Viola.

The year was 1939. I could see Margaret as she sat alone on a street curb inside a rather dusty old European town. At this point in my clairvoyant 'movie' two young boys ran up to Margaret and proceeded to hit her with their fists and spit on her. As she tried to fight off their assault, I saw my client, Viola, as a young schoolgirl. She was making her way home from school with a friend.

Neither of the girls had ever met Margaret. Yet, when Viola and her schoolmate saw what was happening to this Jewish woman, they promptly walked up to her assailants and yelled at them to leave the defenseless woman alone. After suffering the savage beating for a few moments more, the boys finally left.

Still in shock from the cruel attack, Margaret quietly thanked Viola and her friend for defending her. Without saying a word, Viola and her friend quickly left the scene of Margaret's misery.

More than sixty years later and now resting comfortably and at peace on the other side, Margaret wished to thank Viola once again for what she did on her behalf that day.

Viola was moved to tears upon hearing the message. She was humbled at the realization that her gesture six decades earlier had made a difference in the life of a woman she never knew.

Yet, there was something from that day so many years ago that had haunted Viola each day since. Until this moment, she had been unable to forgive herself for it.

Viola told me she had always felt great guilt about not having done anything more for Margaret. Most painful to her was the remembrance that after she shooed the young boys away, she quickly looked around to see if a member of the German Gestapo had seen her come to the aid of the Jewish woman.

"The penalty for such an infraction was death," Viola told me.

I assured her that her reaction was a human response to fear. I then told her that her actions as a young girl on that day were compassionate and very courageous in a time when bravery on behalf of a Jewish person might very well have cost her life.

From her home with God, Margaret promptly agreed and handed Viola a bouquet of her favorite flowers, red roses, as a gesture of her unending gratitude.

Beyond physical time and space, Margaret was able to reach across the veil and deliver not only a thank you, but a message of comfort and peace to a woman haunted by their meeting nearly a lifetime ago.

The communication between Viola and Margaret that day in 2003 still serves as a reminder to me of the importance of our every day encounters with friends and strangers alike.

Take a moment to remember your own clairvoyant experiences:

_____

_____

_____

_____

_____

_____

_____

_____

_____

_____

_____

Clairsentience

Clairsentience means "clear feeling." Have you ever had the feeling that you have been in the presence of an angel? Have you ever felt the presence of a departed loved one and come away with the feeling that they have let you know they are okay on the other side? These feelings are your body's way of receiving Divine communication.

When I am speaking to those on the other side, they sometimes let me know how they passed by letting me 'feel' how their condition or moment of crossing over made them feel. Sometimes it comes in the form of a constriction in my chest or maybe even a sharp pain to my head. In all instances though, they always share the feeling of love and peacefulness of finally stepping out of their physical bodies and back into their purest form; Spirit.

At times, this can be quite dramatic and physically painful.

In the summer of 2004 I had the experience of doing a reading for a woman by the name of Loretta.

Shortly after sitting down, a young man telling me that he was Loretta's son appeared beside her.

After describing this young man to her and giving her a very personal message, Loretta knew that she was definitely in the company of her son.

Telepathically, I asked her son, Vince, how he crossed over. Before I heard an answer however, I felt a powerful blast to my chest which literally threw me back in my chair. I felt a sharp pain and burning sensation from my mid section to my upper body.

I relayed what was happening to Loretta who confirmed that her only son had been murdered a year earlier. He had been shot several times in his chest region.

As in many cases where someone dies a violent death, Vince asked me to let his mother know that he didn't suffer long in his physical body. He wanted her to know that after the first gunshot blast, he stepped out of his physical body. His Spiritual body stood by and watched his corporeal body suffer further gunshot wounds and ultimately, die. Through it all, Vince was unable to feel the physical pain of what was happening to him.

This revelation was an obvious relief to a woman who not only found her son's bloody, bullet riddled body, but to a mother who spent sleepless nights and tormented days worrying that her beloved boy had suffered a long and excruciating death.

This painful, yet cathartic connection with her son gave Loretta the courage that she would need the following day as she took the witness stand in the trial of her son's murderers, who have since been imprisoned for the remainder of their natural lives.

Not all clairsentient experiences are uncomfortable. On the contrary, most are a very warm and reassuring experience.

This is particularly true in the case of Angels.

Many of my clients and students tell me that at different times in their lives they have felt the presence of Angels around them. When I ask them how they knew that they had experienced an angelic visitation, they report feelings of being embraced by a warmth that enveloped their entire body or felt as though they had been wrapped in the loving energy of angelic wings. On some occasions, I hear stories from clients who have actually felt a pressure or weight being lifted off their weary shoulders, simply by asking for angelic help.

Perhaps you've felt the gentle touch of a loved one who has crossed over or simply 'felt' that they were okay. Have you ever felt as though something was going to happen and it did?

Times in my life when I've felt the presence of Spirit:

_____

_____

_____

_____

_____

_____

_____

Clairaudience

Clairaudience means "clear hearing."

Have you ever experienced the sound of music suddenly playing in your head, and thought to yourself, "Where did that come from?"

Take for example, my friend Miriam who, while listening to a church vocalist during one Sunday mass, began to hear as she called it, "the music of the angels" begin to play in her head. Looking around her place of worship to see if the full choir had joined the lone singer from another part of the church, she was surprised to find that there were no other choir members, or church musicians in sight. Despite this fact, Miriam could clearly hear an entire symphony playing ever more loudly.

Long after the vocalist stopped singing, Miriam continued to hear the celestial choir perform their heavenly harmonies within her mind. With tears streaming down her cheeks, she sat in the pew completely enveloped by the blissful music. Her heart told her and her Spirit confirmed that she had been in the presence of Angels.

With a renewed sense of wellness, Miriam left mass knowing that something un-explainable, yet life changing had happened to her. To this day, merely thinking about her private sonata brings tears of joy to her eyes and contentment to her heart.

Our helpers on the other side of the veil have also been known to shout "Look out!" just as an errant vehicle swings into an opposing lane, giving the other driver an opportunity to avoid disaster.

This scenario happened to me. By yelling those words into my left ear, my guides helped me avoid a serious accident with a semi truck whose driver wasn't paying full attention.

When I am speaking to someone on the other side of the veil, they talk to me much in the same way they would have spoken while in their physical body. Regional dialects, foreign languages and favorite phrases are commonly used to help me understand who they are and to help loved ones recognize them.

Some days, Patsy Cline's hit, "Crazy," will begin playing over and over in my mind. When this happens, I know that my aunt Mary Lou is thinking of me.

Each day, many people experience this same phenomena in a way that is unique to the relationship they had with their loved one. Rather than write it off as idle mind chatter, they realize that beyond the grave, a special bond continues between them and their special someone.

Times in my life when I heard Spirit speaking to me:

_____

_____

_____

_____

_____

_____

_____

_____

_____

_____

_____

_____

_____

_____

_____

_____

Clairosmesiance

Clairosmesiance means "clear smelling."

Through our sense of smell, we are able to perceive the presence of Spirit.

The most common of which is to smell a favorite perfume, flowers or cigar of a loved one who has crossed over.

I have had many students and clients tell me that they have experienced the presence of Mary, the Mother of Jesus during prayer. They are assured that they are in the presence of the Holy Mother because they clearly smell the scent of fresh roses in the air.

In some cases, those in spirit will tell me a story through my sense of smell. Whether it is the scent of a roaring camp fire, freshly baked bread or the smell of a fine chardonnay, they speak to me of life experiences which brought them great joy.

At other times, they speak to me of their sorrows or of their passing in this way.

This was the case with Brad. When the wife of Brad's business partner came to see me about his death, I had no idea how he had passed. Before long however, it became apparent that he died of a gunshot wound. As Brad stood before me, I began to smell the scent of gunpowder.

My client confirmed that Brad had indeed been killed by gunfire.

In the case of Tony, a 17 year old victim of a drunk driver, he made me to understand that he had crossed over in this way, by having me smell gasoline and alcohol.

Tony's very distraught mother confirmed that yes, her young son had died at the hands of an intoxicated driver.

As I was attuning her to the second degree of Reiki, Patricia, a long time student, sensed that she was in the company of her maternal grandmother who had crossed over many years earlier. During the attunement ceremony, she could actually smell the sweet aroma of coconut oil in the air around her.

When the process was finished, the other students began to talk about the coconut scent that had filled the room as they were being attuned. They wondered if I had used coconut oils during this portion of the workshop.

After assuring them that I had not, Patricia told everyone that her grandmother had been present during the ceremony, and that she had delivered a very personal and moving message to her.

Patricia went on to tell us that her beloved grandmother had been a revered healer in a remote mountain village in the Philippines, and that coconut scented lotions and oils were her favorite to wear.

Grandmother stepped through the veil of Spirit and into my classroom to congratu-late her granddaughter who is a registered nurse, for continuing to learn new ways of healing. She told Patricia that she was delighted at her participation in the workshop, and that she would continue to walk with her on the healer's journey.

The presence of such an esteemed healer at my Reiki workshop was truly a gift not only to her granddaughter, but to the rest of us as well.

My own clairosmesiant experiences:

_____

_____

_____

_____

_____

_____

_____

_____

Clairgustiance

Clairgustiance means "clear tasting." When this takes place, our taste buds are activated without any physical substance touching them.

Tasting cotton candy might simply be a reminder from the Angels to think about the sweetness and abundance in your life.

Other times, it may be a message from a loved one on the other side.

When spirit speaks to us in this manner, we may experience the sudden taste of chocolate chip cookies, hazelnut coffee, peanut butter, dill pickles or a specific ethnic food. Something that is specifically related to someone who has crossed over.

On one occasion, I was asked to help locate a missing woman who was believed to be dead. Those who were directly involved with solving the case were looking for confirmation of their suspicions.

Their fears were confirmed when she appeared to me in Spirit form, later that day.

After asking the young woman to describe to me how she died, my breathing became labored and I could taste wet rags or socks in my mouth. They tasted as though they were soaked in lake water. At first I felt as though I was drowning and then suddenly everything became peaceful. My body felt light.

The physical sensations suddenly ended and I was left looking at a small, tree-lined lake on my psychic inner screen. The water looked dark and cold. Tomb-like. An overwhelming sense of dread permeated the entire vision.

Sadly, and just as she had explained, this young mother had been gagged with white rags, her mouth taped shut and then thrown into the lake. Her bound body was eventually recovered there several months later.

Years later, her murderer was tried before a jury and brought to justice. For his heinous crime, he is now living his own tomb-like existence within the walls of a prison cell.

My own clairgustiant experiences:

_____

_____

_____

_____

_____

Claircognisance

Claircognisance, also referred to as precognition, this form of spirit communication allows us to see a glimpse of an event yet to come.

Time as we know it here on earth is much different that the reality of time in Spirit. It is due to this fact that we have the ability to catch a quick look at events that we've not yet experienced on the physical plane.

For some, these future snapshots come during dream time, when we are fully relaxed and not consumed by the busy-ness of our day to day lives.

For others, this may happen suddenly while driving or housecleaning. It may even happen while attending one of your children's sporting events.

Right out of the clear blue sky you may see an image of an out of town friend that you've not seen in quite some time. That friend might then call you to let you know they've been thinking of you, and that they are getting married or that they are coming in to town for a visit.

In some cases, you might very well have a vision of someone's passing, only to find out shortly after that the person has indeed crossed over.

These types of spiritual communication can sometimes be unsettling. As a young child, I found them quite upsetting. As I grew older however, I came to understand that my 'spiritual antenna' had the ability to pick up on any sort of psychic information that happened to be roaming about the airwaves, kind of like a CB radio. I also came to understand that I could set boundaries on my gifts. You can too.

If you find that pre-cognitive experiences are overwhelming, you are perfectly right to ask your Angels, Guides or the Creator to please not send images of impending events. While it's a wonderful thing to see future weddings, babies, promotions, awards, etc., it can be a heavy burden to know that someone you love is going to cross over shortly.

In working with Spirit, rest assured that they will help you set boundaries on the information you wish to receive.

Just as it is imperative to set healthy boundaries in your physical life, it is important to set boundaries in your spiritual life as well.

My own claircognisant experiences:

Dreams

Because our days become so filled with the busy-ness of living, Spirit will often speak to us during our dream time. It is during our sleep that we are free to explore Spirit unencumbered by our day to day concerns.

It can be difficult to hear the voice of Spirit when we are in a state of intense grief or stress. Dreamtime offers us respite and an opportunity to clearly encounter our loved ones on the other side of the veil.

Often times I hear stories in which a client has dreamed of a deceased loved one appearing to them with a message letting them know they are safe and at peace on the other side.

One such encounter happened to a client by the name of Regina. She reported to me that her mother came to her in a dream shortly after her physical death. Regina told me that in her dream, her mother was "glowing like an angel." Although her mother didn't speak to her, Regina could feel her mother tell her that she was at peace in heaven. Her mother appeared to her as a much younger woman, radiant and full of life. This made Regina feel that her mother was no longer suffering the effects of old age and that she was full of life once again.

The dream time vision of her mother fully restored and at peace, gave Regina great comfort and solace following the loss of the woman she loved and admired most of all.

Dreams in which visions of future events take place, are sometimes facilitated by Angels, Spirit Guides or loved ones as well. In nearly every case I am asked if I believe that a visitation by Spirit has truly happened. My response to that question is a hearty, "Yes!"

I met my son Dane for the first time, in just this way.

Several months before I became pregnant with Dane, an Angel appeared to me during a dream. In this dream, the angel was holding the hand of a 3 year old boy with fair skin, thick wavy black hair and big brown eyes. He looked like a cherub wearing a suit of navy blue knickers and suspenders. On top of his head was a blue tam o'shanter hat with a bright red ball. His chubby little hands held on tightly to the Guardian Angel at his side.

The angel spoke gently, yet firmly: "Denise, this is your son, Dane! He wishes to be called by this name."

Then the dream ended.

I awoke from my dream and sat in the darkened silence of my bedroom. I knew without question that there was a dark-haired little boy waiting to come to me, and that he wished to be called Dane.

Eleven months later, Dane Andrew arrived. He was crowned with curly black hair and gazed at me through the most beautiful dark brown eyes I had ever seen.

Take a moment to think about the dreams in which you've had personal encounter with Spirit and how those dreams affected you:

_____

_____

_____

_____

_____

_____

_____

_____

_____

_____

_____

Just as messages are given to you in dreams, you may also ask for insight and answers to be revealed to you during your dream time. As you prepare to go to sleep, ask your companions in spirit to speak to you in your dream state. If it doesn't happen the very first time, continue to ask each night until an answer is received.

If you are having the opposite problem, and you are waking up tired each day due to too much dream time activity, ask Spirit to please give you a night off from receiving divine guidance or from doing too much astral traveling.

You may also keep a piece of black obsidian stone next to your bed or under your pillow to help divert too much psychic activity. Many people have told me that having a glass of water on your night stand also helps. Like a lightning bolt attracted to a pool of water, a glass of H_2O will absorb excess psychic energy. Just be sure to flush the water down the commode in the morning rather than drink it!

Dream time questions I have asked and the answers I have received:

Meditation

The fastest way to connect with Spirit is through meditation. By slowing down and going within, we are able to access the divine knowledge that resides within each of us, and are able to go beyond the veil of physical reality to the place within, where infinite wisdom dwells. Through meditation, we are able to quiet our busy minds and tend to this Divine knowledge.

With slow, steady and rhythmic breathing, in through our nose and out through our mouth, our body begins the process of relaxing. The fresh oxygen being brought into our lungs brings balance and nourishment to our body, mind and spirit. Accompanied by guided imagery, we are then able to tap into our imagination and remember things we have always known, and to create a sacred space for Spirit to speak to us. I liken our imagination to a cosmic filter through which Spirit is able to communicate with us in a way that each individual can understand as only their soul can.

For some, complete silence is the form of meditation that offers optimal spirit communication. For others, sitting in silence and concentrating on a single word such as "peace" or "love", brings about clarity and enlightenment.

Meditation can also be done in non-conventional ways such as a walk through nature or a labyrinth. Some people find themselves in a meditative state as they jog, paint, sculpt or even as they wallpaper a room.

During meditation, each individual will experience the presence of Angels and Guides in Spirit in a slightly different way. Some will simply 'feel' their presence. It may feel like a tingling, or perhaps like a warm sweater. It may even come in a feeling like a cool breeze or a tap on the shoulder. Others may 'see' their celestial friends. They may appear as an orb or vision of pure light. The light may be colored, or it may be crystal clear. Others may see their guides in human figure form. Finally, some may 'hear' their divine companions. Celestial music, soft voices or even the sound of an eagle may hearken the presence of your heavenly friends.

Wherever you find yourself relaxed and unencumbered by outside worries or concerns is a form of meditation. Some of my greatest inspirations have come to me while walking my dog, Merlin.

The following guided meditation will take you back to a time long ago when communing with the spirit of nature and the voice of the goddess was part of daily life. This meditation can be found on my guided meditation CD entitled, "Beyond the Veil...Lies a Mystic Journey."

Let us now visit Avalon, a place of enchantment, and magic where the veil between heaven and earth does not exist:

Return to Avalon

Breathe deeply and gently close your eyes.

Exhale and relax your entire body.

Breathe deeply once again and as you exhale, relax your mind.

Breathe deeply once more and as you exhale, go deeply within.

Find yourself on the mystic Isle of Avalon. From high atop the Glastonbury Tor, you can see forever. You can see beyond time.

Feel the cool moist morning air upon your face. Let it refresh your soul.

Feel the earth beneath your feet. You are standing on hallowed ground.

You are at peace here.

Take a look around you now and gaze upon the splendor of this enchanted place. Listen to the sounds of Beltane as the remembrance of it comes to you on the tide of the gentle breeze. Hear the voice of the High Priestess. She has a message for you from long, long ago… Listen…

The rising sun begins to part the mists that delicately cover sleepy Glastonbury below. Let its warmth fill your entire being.

Once parted, the mists reveal the majesty of Glastonbury Abbey. Her hand carved steeples and bell towers rise like angelic beacons high into the blue Celtic sky. Hear the Cathedral Bells as they toll for all time.

This ancient place of worship now speak to you of ages old. If you listen closely you can hear the voices of Arthur and his Queen Guinevere. Hear them as they speak to you from their resting place within the abbey grounds.

The sound of Gregorian chant being sung by abbey monks who once resided in this holy place still fills the air. Feel the energy in their sacred songs of prayer.

As you continue to relax alongside the stone ruins of St. Michael's steeple pay attention to the Wise ones as they speak to you of the hidden Grail. Perhaps they speak to you of YOUR hidden grail. Simply listen.

Off in the distance you can hear the running waters of the Chalice Well. Visualize yourself standing in the healing pool and drinking from the Lions Head Fountain. Feel these magical waters as they refresh your body and your spirit.

It is now time for you to leave the Isle.

Take a moment to thank the ancient ones for speaking to you for sharing their wisdom.

Remembering all that you have heard, and seen and felt, you now return to your physical body and to the sounds within the room.

Breathe deeply now and when you are ready, gently open your eyes.

Take a moment to reflect on any thoughts, feelings, visions or sounds that you may have experienced during this meditation:

_____

_____

_____

_____

_____

_____

                        _____

                        _____

                        _____

                        _____

Ghosts, Poltergeists and Apparitions ... Oh My!

tudents and clients alike, often ask me about the difference between a ghost, a poltergeist and an apparition.

Like most things in my life, I try to keep the answers simple.

A ghost is a visitor from the realm of Spirit. Sometimes a discarnate spirit who once walked the earth plane will stop in for a short time to deliver a message of some sort. Typically, to let their loved ones know that they are safely home with Mother/Father God and with their loved ones on the other side of the veil.

On some occasions, a discarnate spirit may belong to a person with unfinished business here in the physical world. This is one explanation for haunted homes, hotels, crime scenes, etc.. These spirits are bound by a mission they feel compelled to complete on this side of the veil. It may be a case of helping to solve the mystery of their death or catching their own killer.

Often, when a ghost is able to tell their story to someone with the ability to hear them, and their issue is resolved, they are able to move forward on their soul's journey.

I compare it to the drama we can get caught up in during the course of our daily lives. Until clarity is gained in a situation that causes us discord, we often times become bogged down and mired in emotion and ego. When the crisis is resolved however, and peace returns to our life, we are able to move ahead.

Following the tragic events of September 11, 2001, I was visited by a man who died in the horrific drama that unfolded at the Pentagon.

On September 12th, a disheveled and dust covered young man appeared to me while I was sitting at my desk.

His wire rimmed glasses sat crooked on the bridge of his nose. A portion of the right side of his body was missing.

"Denise, please tell me what has happened to me." he begged.

"I can't find my body. Where is my body?" he asked in a frenzied voice.

Very calmly, I asked him if he had been at the Pentagon the previous day. He told me that yes, he worked at the Pentagon. One moment he had been in his office near the filing cabinet and the next thing he remembered was a loud explosion. Now, he was searching for his body. He didn't feel 'right.'

Carefully and with as much detail as I was aware of, I explained to this confused soul, all of the events surrounding the terrorist attack upon the Pentagon. My boss had been just miles away at a conference, when all hell broke loose in Washington, D.C. I suspected that this puzzled soul found his way to me through my association with someone who had been in the area of the calamity, too. In this case, it was the man I worked for.

He listened intently and with great sadness on his once handsome face, as I spoke.

Very gently, I continued, "You no longer need your physical body, because you are now in your perfect spiritual body. It's time for you to go home to God."

"Will you help me, Denise?" he asked in a pleading manner.

"Yes," was all I could muster in my own trembling voice.

Together he and I called out to the Light of the Creator to guide him safely home. While doing so, I watched as he began to slowly fade from my sight.

"Thank you, Denise! I promise that I will let you know that I made it okay," were his last words to me.

The next morning, I looked at photos of the victims of the terrorist attacks as they became available on the internet. Just as he promised, I came upon a photo of a smiling young man with light brown hair and dark, gentle eyes. This time, his thin metal rimmed glasses sat perfectly in place on is very handsome face.

"Thank you, Denise. I made it home. I'm with my Grandfather," I could hear the peace in his voice now.

With a whisper I responded, "You're very welcome. Thank you for letting me know."

Most ghostly encounters happen for me just as they did in the previous story. However, some haunted homes are inhabited by spirits who are simply attached to their life as it was during their earthly existence.

If, as I believe, it is true that we create our own reality, I've come to believe that some people simply like the reality that they created in the physical plane and plan to enjoy it into eternity.

On occasion I will get a phone call from someone who would like to get rid of a ghost that has taken up residence in their house. According to the ghost however, it is my client who has taken up residence in their house.

In cases like these there are usually a few realistic options.

1.   Everyone plays nice and gets along under the same roof.
2.   The ghost leaves.
3.   The homeowner leaves.

It's just that simple.

If no consensus is reached and the butting of heads ensues, we might then encounter what I term a poltergeist.

A far cry from the mild mannered ghost who just wishes to be acknowledged, a spirit who is fending off what it feels is a squatter or threat to their territory, can be a cantankerous hooligan.

Objects that go sailing across a room, slamming doors and nasty smells may indicate the presence of a poltergeist. Like a spoiled child throwing a hissy fit, these disembodied spirits want everyone to notice them and acquiesce to their demands. They create fear by intimidation.

On some occasions, a poltergeist might just 'stop in' to raise a little ruckus.

This is precisely what happened to me the night I was awakened by the sound of the steel door which leads from my kitchen into my garage opening and then slamming shut over and over again.

Angrily, I rolled out of bed, put my leopard print slippers on my feet and stormed down the staircase with a 'clippity clop,' into the kitchen.

"Okay, you got my attention!" was how I began the conversation.

Standing beside my white refrigerator, I watched the heavy steel door heave open and shut with a thunderous boom. In the chilly air, I could feel the presence of a ghostly menace who was challenging my courage to stand up to it.

Call it mother bear instinct, my triple Scorpio nature or good old fashioned fury, I pointed my right index finger in the direction of the cranky specter and said with a growl, "IF, you know what is good for you, you will leave *right now* before I really get mad. Cuz if I get *really* mad, I will call on every Angel of Light, and Christ Light presence throughout the Universe, to kick your sorry butt out of my house and away from my family! *Now leave this place*!"

With a final heave, the door once again opened wide and with a loud bang, slammed shut.

Still angry about the intrusion, I mumbled to myself and anyone who could hear me on the other side and 'clippity clopped,' all the way back upstairs. I removed my leopard print slippers and climbed back in to bed.

"The gall of some people!" were my last thoughts as I drifted back to sleep.

Reflecting on the experience the following morning made me laugh.. I hoped that none of my neighbors had been up and about at the same time. Had they been looking through my kitchen windows, I'm quite certain they would have found my poltergeist experience quite entertaining or a bit unnerving.

What a sight I must have been!

Oh well, I told myself, it was just one more episode in the life of a modern day mystic.

When working with cranky spirits, I always remind myself that, "The Light shatters darkness and love always wins."

If you should ever encounter an unruly spirit and your requests to have them leave do not work, or you feel ill-equipped to handle the situation, I recommend that you seek the help of a professional. Call upon a skilled psychic medium, Feng Shui master, shaman, minister, priest/ess, etc. to help in the process.

On the other end of the ethereal spectrum, are apparitions. To me, they are the kinder, gentler, form of ghostly appearances.

Prayer and meditation often facilitate these types of visitations. When we connect our heart and spirit to the Source of Creation via quiet contemplation, we may encounter a visit from a loved one, a saint or an ascended master.

An example of this happened to me while I was deep in prayer and meditation for physical healing.

With my eyes closed, sitting in lotus position in the center of my candlelit meditation room, I could feel a presence begin to manifest. As I waited patiently for the apparition to fully appear, I began to thank Mother/Father God for what I could feel was taking place.

Before long, I opened my eyes and experienced the spiritual presence of Jesus sitting in lotus position directly in front of me.

Total peace filled the air around me and permeated every living cell within me. It was magnificent.

Within a few short moments, the apparition was gone. The sense of peace however, stayed with me long after the vision ended.

Now and again, life changing messages from Spirit come to us in words. From time to time, however, they come in simple, yet powerful feelings.

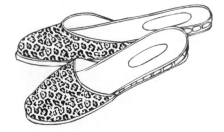

"The intuitive mind is a sacred gift and the rational mind is a faithful servant. We have created a society that honors the servant and has forgotten the gift."

Albert Einstein, (1879—1955), German-born American
Physicist, Nobel Prize Winner 1921

Preparing for Sacred Work Inviting the Light and Creating Sacred Ceremony

efore you begin meditation, or any type of sacred work, be sure to invite your celestial companions to join you as you seek Divine Guidance. Call upon your Angels, Spirit Guides, and Totem Animals to be with you. Light a candle and give thanks for the company of these teachers and for the divine guidance you are about to receive. Just as we appreciate a thank-you, so too do our heavenly companions.

You may also use a bit of incense or essential oils to balance the energy of your sacred space. I recommend rose, copal, sandalwood or frankincense and myrrh. The essence of these scents carries a very high vibration. As their vibration is released into the air, it dissipates any lower vibrations that may be in the area and at the same time raises the vibration to a level conducive to spiritual work.

Some prefer to use Tibetan or crystal singing bowls to raise the vibrational frequency in a room. Tingsha's are also useful in dispersing lower vibrations and bringing in higher vibrations. Yet others use the ancient method of toning. Several heartfelt "OM's" will immediately set the energy of a room and of your own energy field and prepare you for divine guidance. OM is the Sanskrit word meaning "God".

Following this, you must take a moment to 'ground' or 'balance' yourself. What is grounding and balancing?

Grounding is firmly connecting yourself to the physical realm, such as Mother Earth. You can do this by visualizing tree roots growing out of the bottoms of your feel and going deep down into Mother Earth. Remember when you are finished to bring the tree roots up out of Mother Earth. If you are outdoors you can ground yourself by hugging a tree or by putting your hands in soil.

Balancing is about equalizing the energy in and around your body. This energy is known as the "chakra" system and the "aura". Chakra is a Sanskrit word meaning "wheels of energy". These wheels of energy are located along your spine, your forehead

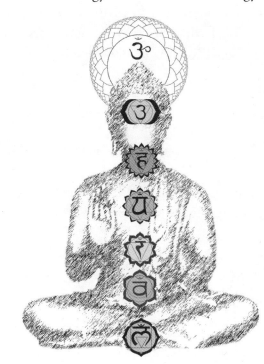

and the top of your head. Your aura field is the field of energy, which surrounds or encases your entire body.

First, take a moment to center yourself by breathing deeply through your nose and exhaling completely, out through your mouth. Do this three times, or in multiples of three. The number three is the number of Universal Creativity. When we think of sun, moon and stars or earth, wind and fire, we see this cosmic pattern of threes.

As you continue to breathe in this rhythmic fashion, you may wish to balance your chakras before proceeding or to visualize yourself surrounded in a shimmering crystal white light.

Chakras

The most common teachings regarding chakras center on the philosophy of seven chakra centers located along your body's energy meridians. They are from bottom to top:

1st Chakra – Color: Red
Located at the base of the spine. This energy center represents your seat of security and survival. It connects you to Mother Earth and is home to Kundalini energy. Burning some cedar or clove essential oil will enhance and balance this chakra.

2nd Chakra – Color: Orange
Located just below the navel. This energy center represents creativity – procreation, sexuality, and is the center through which 'clear feeling' or clairsentience enters our consciousness. Burning some ylang-ylang or sandalwood will help enhance and balance this chakra.

3rd Chakra – Color: Yellow
Located just above the navel. This energy center represents our will, autonomy and self esteem. Burning some lavender, rosemary and bergamot essential oils will help enhance and balance this chakra.

4th Chakra – Color: Green
Located in the heart center. This energy center represents the energy of love. The love

that we have for ourselves and the love that we have for others. This is the chakra of compassion. Burning some Rose essential oil will help enhance and balance this chakra.

5th Chakra – Color: Sky blue
Located at the base of the throat. This energy center is about 'speaking our truth'. It is also the center through which 'clear hearing' or clairaudience enters our consciousness. Burning some sage or eucalyptus essential oils will help enhance and balance this chakra.

6th Chakra – Color: Indigo
Located in the center of the forehead. This energy center is about 'seeing things clearly'. It is the center through which 'clear seeing' or clairvoyance enters our consciousness. Burning some mint or jasmine essential oils will help enhance and balance this chakra.

7th Chakra – Color: Purple, Silver, and Gold
Located at the crown of the head. This energy center is the gateway and our connection to the Divine. Seen as a golden halo or aura in many forms of sacred art, this seventh chakra is our connection to our Divine Home. Burning olibanum or lotus essential oils will help enhance and balance this chakra.

By visualizing each of your chakras, beginning at the base of your spine and moving gently upward, vibrantly spinning in perfect balance, you help to keep your wheels of energy in perfect alignment. Being in balance helps you receive, understand and then act upon psychic guidance.

You can also maintain balance by drinking a lot of water, eating healthy food and getting plenty of rest. All of these things help keep your psychic 'antenna' clean and in perfect operating condition.

Protecting Your Aura

Because our aura can become cluttered with the emotions, problems and outside psychic influences (psychic attack) of others throughout our day, an easy way to keep your aura clean is to take a bath in Epsom salts before bed. Be sure to get your head wet too. This way, negative energy doesn't simply move upward, causing a nasty headache! By adding a little lavender to your bath, not only is your aura cleaned, but it is also relaxed.

Envisioning your body and aura completely surrounded by crystal white light during the day is an excellent way to protect yourself from low vibrations as well. Keeping a piece of black obsidian nearby will also help to absorb negativity.

Just as you can smudge a room to clear negativity, you can also smudge your body and your aura. After lighting a high vibration incense or sage/sweetgrass in a fire safe burner, allow the smoke to begin to billow out of the burner . As it does, fan the billowing smoke with a feather so that you in effect, bathe yourself in the essence of the incense.

Ultimately, always remember that 'like attracts like'. If you indulge in high vibration activities such as positive speech, meditation, prayer, volunteer work, and group activities involving people of integrity, you will continue to attract high vibration experiences in your life. The positive energy that you exude in your thoughts or daily activities will come back to you as positive energy in the form of positive experiences, people and abundance.

Likewise, when we spend our time in the company of people of less integrity who spend much of their time gossiping, living in a constant state of fear, greed, complaining, using illegal substances, and hanging out in low vibration places, we will continue to attract those experiences in our lives. When we put forth negative energy, we shall attract negativity in return. Separating ourselves from these people and activities will increase our vibration and heighten our ability to ward off psychic attack and negativity in our lives.

By paying attention to our own energy and the energy of others, we begin to notice the subtleties of how our aura and chakras come into play. A red aura can certainly describe someone who is "red with anger". When someone says they are feeling gray, you can be sure that their aura reflects their gloomy outlook. When someone is operating their life with clear intention, rest assured that their chakras and their aura is exuding all of the crystal clear colors of the rainbow.

A fun way to take a look at your own aura is to stand in a dimly lit room in front of a mirror and to simply let your eyes relax as you gaze at the figure of yourself. Your aura may appear as quick little flashes of colored light at first or perhaps a soft glow. Simply pay attention to the way you feel and to the light that you are radiating. And, as they say, practice makes perfect. Keep on looking and you will be amazed to find that before long, you will be seeing the aura around others!

Creating a Sacred Altar

Does the smell of sandalwood incense and the mystical sound of Tibetan temple bells take your Spirit to another place or time? Does the mesmerizing beat of Native American drums and the smell of sweet grass send your spirit soaring? If the answer is yes, you are not alone. These scents and these sounds touch a part of our soul that longs to participate in ancient ceremony. It touches our very essence, reminding us of our connection to All That Is.

Instead of traveling thousands of miles to the Far East or to the American Southwest, you can create these sacred moments within your own home or even in your back yard garden. It's fun and it's easy.

You'll need just a few things to get started:

> Small table/dresser or bench
> Candles
> Incense
> Sacred Object/Photo

Start by placing your table/altar in a place where you will be able to spend prayerful meditative time undisturbed. I keep mine in my meditation room near a window facing my fairy garden and bird feeders. I like the feeling of Mother Nature taking part in my daily meditations. Some people prefer to have fresh flowers on their altar for the same reason.

As you put your altar together, set forth your intention to make this a sacred place of reflection. You can even do this out loud, asking your angels and guides or god/goddess for assistance. Our many helpers in the realm of Spirit are more than happy to take part in such an auspicious occasion.

Placing a lovely piece of cloth on your altar is a nice way to begin making it sacred. This cloth may simply be a particular color and fabric that you are fond of, or perhaps as elaborate as a painting on silk. Choose something that makes you feel as though you are truly in a sacred space. You are!

Candles are a must. At least one candle should be present on your altar. By lighting a candle, you are asking the Light of the Creator to be present in your time of prayer. The candle flame represents the element of Fire.

Stones represent the element of Earth. Once they have been cleansed in light of the sun or under cool running water, crystals and stones are a terrific way of bringing positive, grounding energy to your sacred space.

Don't forget to add an Air element such as a feather to your altar. It may be a feather from your favorite type of bird, or perhaps a feather you found on a special outing.

A vessel of holy water, water from a sacred well, or water which you have blessed and placed in a bowl is also very important to your altar. The element of Water represents Spirit and our ability to traverse the waters of the divine mysteries.

A photo or statue of an Angel, Totem Animal or Spiritual Master will bring the energy of that divine being into your room and into your sacred work. They can also serve as a focal point for your wandering mind during meditation. Choose one, or choose several that resonate with your sense of Spirit.

Incense or essential oils of sandalwood, copal, rose, or frankincense and myrrh are wonderful tools for keeping your sacred space clear of any negative energy. It prepares the way for clear communication with your Angels, Guides and the Creator.

Ultimately, your sacred altar should serve as a reminder of your connection to the Creator and a place where you can go to your Temple Within for daily contemplation, healing and renewal.

Take a moment to imagine your sacred altar:

Where I will locate my altar: _____

Why did I choose this spot? _____

The altar itself will be made of: _____

A special cloth made of _____ will dress my altar.

Candles I would like to have on my altar _____

The element of Earth will be represented by: _____

The element of Water will be represented by: _____

The element of Air will be represented by: _____

Angel(s) that I would like to include: _____

Why? _____

Ascended Master(s) I would like to include: _____

Why? _____

Totem Animal(s) I would like to include: _____

Why? _____

Stone energies I would like to include: _____

Why? _____

Other Sacred Objects I would like to have included and why I have chosen them:

1. _____

_____

2. _____

_____

3. _____

_____

4. _____

_____

Out with the Old, In with the New

"As within, so without." That age-old saying is very important when it comes to the mystic journey. Just as our personal energy fields become cluttered, so do our homes and offices. As you begin to embrace your psychic self, it is important to get rid of old unwanted and no longer needed clutter from the spaces that you occupy.

When we think of the mystics from times past, we realize that most of them lived a very austere life. There were no kitchen drawers overflowing with junk or stacks of old newspapers or magazines lying about. Neither did they have clothes hanging in their closets that date back to high school!

Whether we realize it or not, we spend lots of time thinking about our piles of junk and unwanted stuff. Not to mention the Feng Shui faux paux they create! By eliminating the "things" in life that no longer serve our higher self, we quite literally make room for the new things that have been trying to come to us, including spiritual guidance.

If we are consumed with thinking that we should organize our kitchen cupboards, closets and the spaces under our beds, yet never get around to it, we are wasting lots of valuable energy that could be focused on our soul path. It's difficult to hear the voices of our guides and angels when we're too busy thinking about having so many pairs of shoes that we can't close our closet doors any longer.

Whether you create a clearing out ceremony that takes you weeks to complete or you choose to clean out the old in one fell swoop, you will notice an immediate difference in the world around you and in your ability to communicate with Spirit.

The most important thing is to just buckle up and begin the process. By clearing one drawer, one closet, or one room at a time, you will be amazed by how good you feel and how light and airy your home begins to feel.

Following is a list of the areas we tend to collect and hold on to our old junk.

"Out with the old" check off list:

Bedroom(s)
  Closets
  Drawers
  Under the bed
  Piles in the corner

Kitchen
  Cupboards
  Countertops
  Drawers
  Appliances
  Piles in the corner

Living Room(s)
  Under furniture
  Table tops
  Piles in the corner

Storage Room
  Shelves

Office
  Desk
  File Cabinets
  Closet
  Credenza

Laundry Room
  Cabinets
  Closet
  Drawers

Bathroom(s)
  Counter tops
  Vanities
  Outdated medicine
  Old makeup and toiletries
  Cabinets
  Broken hair dryers, curling irons
  Linen closet
  Piles in the corner

Garage
  Car(s)
  Boat(s)
  RV(s)
  Workbench
  Shelves
  Cabinets

Mud Room

Hallway Closets

Cupboards

Workout Room

Deck

Porch

Storage Shed

Other areas that need to be cleared of clutter:

1. _____

2. _____

3. _____

4. _____

5. _____

6. _____

7. _____

8. _____

9. _____

10. _____

To Everything There is a Season

The mystic journey also brings with it, new friends, new teachers, new colleagues. Life is truly never the same once you have embarked upon the journey of the soul.

You will find a gentle shedding of people in your life as your travel forward on your spiritual path. Every person we meet, every person we interact with and love brings the gift of life lessons. Each of these lessons represents a season in your life. Some of these seasons will last a lifetime and others just a short period of time, perhaps just hours.

Outdated belief systems that you have had about yourself and about the world around you will also begin to fall away from you. What you were told to believe as a child is not necessarily the truth of who you are today. Yet, we sometimes hang on to hurtful nicknames, religious beliefs and playground events as though they are absolute truths, never to be changed.

In every case, bless the lesson and bless the person who has brought it to you. And when the lesson is complete, bless the separate paths that must be taken.

As you let go, remember to thank the Universe and the Creator of All for the new lessons and new messengers who are coming your way.

Take a moment to think about those things that you are now ready to let go of and why:

_____

_____

_____

_____

New people, adventures, thoughts and beliefs I now wish to experience in my life:

_____

_____

_____

_____

_____

_____

Guides, Gatekeepers and Teachers Oh, and Don't Forget the Faeries

Master Guides

ur Master Guide is that guide in spirit who helps to oversee our spiritual development. This Master Guide is with you during your entire lifetime and in many cases, works with you throughout several lifetimes. Your Master Guide is the one who arranges other guides in spirit to come into your life as needed. Invite your Master Guide to be with you each day as you travel the mystic's journey.

I first met my Master Guide, Enid, while in meditation. This lovely 14th century

Scottish woman has worked with me in many lifetimes. She sees to it that I encounter the right teachers in the spiritual realm and on earth, who will provide the correct course of study, at the appropriate time and at the proper pace in my spiritual development.

Often, when I ask Enid to let me know that I am on the right path or have made a correct decision, she will send a positive affirmation in the way of a beautiful white dove, or the music of Enya or Loreena McKennitt playing on the radio.

Guides

Throughout our many lifetimes, Spirit Guides come into our life for a very short period of time as we learn and grow. They appear just long enough to assure us that we are on the 'right path' or to deliver an important and timely message.

Gatekeepers

Our Gatekeepers are those guides in spirit who accompany us any time we do spiritual work. As the name suggests, they open the gate and stand guard between the physical plane and the spiritual plane. They serve as interpreters, helping us understand spiritual information as it is given to us and serve to keep us safe on our journey. Your Gatekeeper may be an Angel, an Ascended Master, or perhaps another enlightened soul, such as a Native American Shaman who once lived on the earth plane. Some have even encountered a nature spirit as their Gatekeeper.

Whether I am doing work as a psychic medium or teaching a class in metaphysics, Nakoma is always there to help me interpret information from Spirit and to make sure that I am protected from negativity while doing so.

Several years ago, I had a gentleman ask me if I could get in touch with a particular spirit on the other side. I could clearly see the spirit he was talking about, and yet Nakoma forbade me to come in contact with this being. He explained to me that this spirit would not want to leave my presence and would severely drain my energy. He put his arms across his chest and told me adamantly that this would not be allowed.

When I explained this to my client, he told me that he understood; that he had been told this before. In this case, the spirit that my client wished to hear from was quite powerful and not entirely cooperative when asked to leave.

It was a very important lesson in always inviting my Gatekeeper to be present with me when traversing the realm of Spirit.

Teachers

Teachers are those guides in spirit who step into our lives to help us accomplish a specific task or a specific field of learning. For instance, if you desire to pursue a Buddhist path, you may very well find yourself in the company of Siddhartha to lead you to the proper teachers, reading materials, classes, etc. to help you pursue Buddhism. Always invite your Spiritual Teachers to accompany you when pursuing spiritual studies.

My spiritual Teacher, David, was a former member of the Knights Templar. David came into my life at a time when I felt I was ready to take the next step in my spiritual education. While standing in my kitchen one evening, he appeared to me dressed in military regalia once worn by medieval servants of the crown. When I asked him his purpose for appearing to me he replied, "My name is David. I am a loyal member of the Order of the Knights Templar. I am here to take you to the next level of your development."

After thanking David for agreeing to assist me in this manner, he went on to tell me that I would be receiving an invitation to participate in a sacred ceremony.

In a solemn voice befitting that of a Knight of the Realm, he said, "Upon receiving this invitation, Dana, you must agree to attend. I will accompany you."

With that statement, he was gone.

Alone once again, I stood in my kitchen wondering where spirit was leading me. The endless possibilities filled my soul with excitement and anticipation.

It wouldn't take long to find what was planned.

Three days later I received an invitation, just as David had described. It was a call to attend the Isis Ordinations, being held at a convent in the city.

Taking a leap of faith that I had understood David clearly and this was a path I needed to follow, I agreed to attend.

What I and 21 others experienced, was a magnificent day filled with contemplative prayer and learning. The time we spent participating in ancient Egyptian healing and meditation techniques was fascinating.

The highlight of the entire day, however, was the Ordination Rites. Still to this day, it has proven to be one of the most profound events in my life.

As evening began to appear, our teacher started to make preparations for the process of ordination. All 22 of us were about to be ordained as a priest or priestess in the Initiate Order of the Temple of Isis. Each member of our new Order was being called by Spirit to carry out compassionate service to all of humanity. We were being asked by Mother/Father God to serve in our own unique way. Above all else, we were being asked to love one another as we would have another love us. In other words, to be a living example of The Golden Rule.

I liked those marching orders and could hardly wait for the ceremony to begin.

As our teacher lit candles around the room, the sacred space we had created became bathed in a golden glow. The smell of sacred incense filled the air. It was time for the ordinations to begin.

One by one, our teacher called us forward and sat us down upon a beautifully carved chair. She then administered the ordination rites. Soon, it was my turn.

After seating myself upon the ornate chair that felt somehow like a throne, a gold lame' mantle was gentle draped around my shoulders and my forehead anointed with Egyptian oils. Like the others who had gone before me, our instructor whispered a specific message from spirit into my ear. It is something that I shall never forget.

In a soft, almost other-worldly voice, I heard the words, "Dana, remember that you are loved, and that we know you by name. Thank you for answering the call to serve humanity."

With tears welling in my eyes, I looked down at my nametag which was firmly attached to the upper right side of my shirt. It said, 'Denise."

In that moment, I knew that my heart, and my teacher, David, had led me to the proper place.

Imagine my delight when I discovered the next day, that the worldwide organization known as the Fellowship of Isis, is housed in moss covered castle in Scotland. A castle that once belonged to the Order of the Knights Templar.

While I do not pretend to be a saint, I try to live by the vow of compassionate service that I took on that very special day in the year 2000. When I do anything less than that, my Knight in Shining Armor steers me in the right direction.

The Ascended Masters

Also known as Avatars, the list of Ascended Masters is long. These fully enlightened Masters once walked the Earth and continue to guide us from their home amongst the heavens.

Following is a very short list of some of the most often referred to Ascended Masters:

Lord Buddha – the Enlightened One, Indian Mystic and Founder of Buddhism.
Jesus of Nazareth – Also known as Joshua Ben Joseph and Sananda. His life and teachings form the basis of Christianity.
Muhammad – Arab Teacher and Prophet of Islam.
Mary, the Mother of Jesus – Represents the Universal Divine Feminine.
Lord Krishna – Hindu Prophet, The 8th avatar of Vishnu.
Sai Baba – Hindu Holy Man and Prophet
Buddha Maitreya – the Buddha yet to come.
Abraham – Patriarch of the Hebrew people.
Moses – Hebrew Prophet who led the Israelites out of Egypt.
Kuan Yin – Represents the Divine Feminine in Buddhism.
Black Elk – Sioux Prophet and Medicine Man
The Saints – Persons officially recognized by the Church as capable of interceding for people on earth.

Such as:
- St. Andrew
- St. Anthony of Padua
- St. Ann
- St. Bernard of Clairvaux
- St. Christopher
- St. Claire
- St. Francis of Assisi
- St. Catherine of Sienna
- St. John of the Cross

For as long as I can remember, I have been speaking with and listening to the voice of Spirit. And, for as long as I can remember, people have been asking me, "Denise, how do you do this? Is this something that everyone can do?"

For many years, I was unable to explain just how I was able to see and hear Spirit. I just did it. And while some spiritual experiences are simply beyond verbal explanation, I have come to realize that speaking to Spirit is perfectly natural and yes, everyone can do it.

Sometimes, the simplicity of silence provides the best means for hearing the voice of Spirit.

Take a moment now to set a sacred space. In the silence of this holy space, ask all your Guides to come forward and speak to you. You may ask them for insight into a concern, or to simply give you a message for the day. Remember that this message may come in many forms. Simply pay attention to what you see, feel and hear:

Angels

He will give his angels
charge of you,
To guard you in all
your ways.
On their hands they will
will bear you up,
Lest you dash your foot
against a stone.

~Psalm 91:10-11

What are angels? The idea of guardian spirits dates back to early civilization and can be found in the belief systems of cultures around the world. The ancient Assyrians, Greeks, Japanese, Indians and Egyptians are just a few examples of civilizations that had names of individual spirits that watched over and guided every human being.

The existence of angels is an essential element to the four monotheistic religions of the western world: Christianity, Islam, Judaism, and Zoroastrianism. The sacred texts belonging to these faiths teach their followers that angels are as real as the God they serve.

"Angel": From the Greek world "Angelos,"
a translation of the Hebrew word "Malakh," originally meaning "Messenger"

Jacob left Beersheba and went toward Haran. He came to a certain place and stayed there for the night, because the sun had set. Taking one of the stones of the place, he put it under his head and lay down in that place. And he dreamed that there was a ladder set up on the earth, the top of it reaching to heaven; and the angels of God were ascending and descending on it.

~Genesis 28:10

"I am well aware that many will say that no-one can possibly speak with the spirits and angels so long as he is living in the body....But I am deterred by none of these; for I have seen, I have heard, I have felt."

~Swedish Mystic Emanuel Swedenborg

"I looked up at the clouds, and two men were coming there, headfirst like arrows slanting down; and as they came, they sang a sacred song and the thunder was like drumming.

I will sing it for you. The song and the drumming were like this:

"Behold a sacred voice is calling you; all over the sky a sacred voice is calling."

~Black Elk, Lakhota Holy Man

"We look at it and we do not see it;

Its name is The Invisible.

We listen to it and do not hear it;

Its name is The Inaudible.

We touch it and do not find it;

Its name is The Subtle.

~Lao-Tzu, Tao Te Ching, 14

Metatron – Also known as Enoch in the Old Testament. This very large and mighty angel is said to preside over the entire Heavenly Host of Angels.

Archangels

Michael – "Who is like God" or He who looks like God." He is often referred to as St. Michael, the protector of police officers and soldiers. Michael is the defender of Light and goodness.

Gabriel – "Hero of God" or "God is my strength." Gabriel is the angel known for telling the Virgin Mary of her impending birth of Jesus and who later delivered the "Behold, I bring you good tidings of great Joy," news about the newborn Jesus. Gabriel is the messenger who delivered the Koran to Mohammed.

Uriel – "Light of God." Uriel brings Divine Light into our lives. Uriel helps us fulfill our dreams and our goals, while helping us to let go and heal the past. Uriel helps to teach us about forgiveness of ourselves and of others.

Raphael – "God Heals." Raphael is the angel of all healing. He watches over the healing of the planet earth and those who live upon planet earth. Raphael guides those in the healing arts. Call upon Raphael when you or someone you care for needs healing of the body, mind or spirit. Raphael is also the angel of travelers. As you travel the Mystic Journey, remember to call upon him.

The Nine Orders of Angels

Seraphim – These are the closest to the throne of God. They are creatures of pure love and Light.

Cherubim – These are the first angels named in the Bible as God stations them at the gates of Eden. The Cherubim are angels of knowledge and glory as well as guardians of the fixed stars. They are also the celestial record keepers.

Thrones – These are the ministering angels of justice. The Thrones are the first group of angels existing closely to the material realm.

Dominions – These angels supervise other angels and oversee the daily happenings of the Universe. Dominions are the guardians of nations.

Virtues – These are the angels of grace and valor. Their primary purpose is to perform miracles on Earth. They intervene and provide courage and strength in humans during moments of great fear and difficulty.

Powers – These are said to be the first angels created by God. They are protectors against evil on Earth and throughout the cosmos.

Principalities – These angels are said to watch over the leaders of nations, helping them to make wise decisions. They are protectors of religion and help humankind maintain their faith.

Archangels – Messengers bearing divine decrees. Michael, Raphael, Gabriel and Uriel.

Angels – These are the angels closest to human beings. They are intermediaries between the heavenly realm and the earthly realm, between the Creator and humans.

My first encounter with an Angel on earth happened in Chicago in January of 2003. I was invited to speak and sign books at a bookstore in the city. Prior to signing copies of my book, I was asked to lead participants on a guided meditation to meet their angels. Every table in the café was full; there were rows of chairs lined up behind the tables. People were standing in the book aisles. Even before I began the meditation, everyone in that store could 'feel' the presence of Angels. They were drawn to the café like butterflies to a flower.

Although the tables were full, there was one table, which was occupied by a single person. This man appeared to be about 70 years old. He was perhaps 6'3" tall, with beautiful white hair coifed like Albert Einstein. His clothes were rumpled, his hands looked tired, and he had the most beautiful azure blue eyes I have ever seen. As I looked into his eyes I clearly heard that age old saying from Hebrews 13:2; "Do not neglect to show hospitality to strangers, for thereby some have entertained angels unawares." I immediately flashed back to that very morning, when I invited my angel, Enoch, to be with me in Chicago.

As I began to speak and answer questions from the audience, he very gently raised his hand and said "Tell me Denise, do Angels die?"

To which I responded "No, they are eternal, just like we are."

He nodded his head in affirmation and gave me a beautiful smile. A short time later he raised his hand once again and said, "Tell me Denise, do Angels really have wings?"

I answered him with, "If that is how you choose to perceive them. Some people simply feel the presence of their Angels. While other people hear celestial music, others see beautiful orbs or flashes of Light."

He smiled and said "Very good answer."

And just before I prepared to lead the meditation he asked one final question, "Tell me Denise, are all Angels male?"

To which I replied, "Angels are Beings of pure Light. They are pure Love made manifest in Light. They are neither male nor female. It is our own human perception that makes them so."

Enoch sat back in his chair and with a twinkle in his eye said, "Very good Denise."

"Thank you." I responded.

"No, thank you for coming here tonight."

During the cab ride back from the bookstore to the restaurant, my dear friend Chris asked me what I thought of the old rumpled guy sitting at the table by himself.

Before I could respond however, she said, "You know, Denise, that was not an old man sitting there. That was an angel. We could feel his presence and we could feel the energy being exchanged between the two of you. He was your angel making his presence known to you in a very profound way."

I told Chris that I was immediately aware of who he truly was and how blessed I was to have had that very profound and moving experience.

More than ever before, parents are bringing their young children to see me. Trying to discern the spiritual experiences of children can be quite a task for a parent who has not ever faced such things personally.

Two of my very favorite children belong to Tamara, one of my long time students. Chase, who is 10 and Maya who is 6 came into this world like many other children in their generation. Both of them are highly gifted with spiritual sight and knowledge. They clearly see angels and spiritual guides, where their parents see nothing at all. They clearly hear spirit when their parents hear only silence.

The first time I met Maya at the ripe old age of 5, I was taken with her large, crystal blue eyes and her shiny, almost white golden hair. Tamara called to schedule an appointment for Maya so that she could talk to me about the things she hears and sees. She wanted to tell me about how they sometimes scared her, but mostly how they comforted her.

Arriving for their scheduled appointment, Maya greeted me in a way I shall never forget. Dressed in a new floral frock, white sandals and pink fingernail polish, Maya stood in my doorway beaming from ear to ear. "Denise, I'm so happy to be here. I've always wanted to meet someone like me."

As a child I learned to keep experiences to myself. They seemed to confuse and scare everyone around me, more than they confused and scared myself. I couldn't help but think about how wonderful it would have been for me to have had someone to talk to who would have understood.

After entering my home and settling comfortably into the soothing energy of my meditation room, Tamara simply listened as Maya spoke calmly about the beautiful angels that come and sit on her bed with her each night.

Maya began by saying, "The angels never scare me, Denise. They make me feel happy. I like it when they come to see me. Sometimes, the faces in the car scare me, though."

"Do the angels speak to you, Maya?" I asked.

"Sometimes they say words, but mostly they just look at me and smile." was Maya's softly spoken reply.

I then broached the subject of the faces in the car. "Tell me what the faces in the car look like, Maya."

"They're mean," she said.

"What makes them look mean?" I asked.

"Their eyes look mean and sad," was her response.

She continued, "I see them when we're driving in the car. Every time I look in the window I see them. Daddy didn't believe me before, but now he does."

"Do the faces in the window ever say anything to you?" I asked.

Maya responded, "No, they just look at me with their mouths open. But they don't talk."

Remembering my own experiences at the age of 5 and how they terrified me, I told Maya that she could tell the faces to go away. No one had been there to tell me that I had the power to make them go away. Night time wouldn't have been so frightening if there had been. I went on to tell Maya that people in spirit understand that we can see them and that is why they try to get our attention. I told her however, that just because we can see them doesn't mean that they have permission to barge into our space.

"Maya, I said, If the faces that you see make you uncomfortable, just tell them you don't wish to see them. They will understand and they will leave."

Being able to tell Maya that she could set boundaries on her visitors made me feel good. She was visibly relieved to know that her unwanted visitors could be asked to leave. Maya much preferred her beautiful, winged angels. Each night at bedtime, their loving smiles assured her that all was well in her world.

During the course of the rest of our conversation Maya shared with me that she sees bright colors around people. She described them as beautiful rainbows. Talking about auras with such a young child was so refreshing. It made me feel like a kid again!

Ultimately, I assured Maya that her spiritual abilities were indeed a gift from God. I explained that everyone in the world is given gifts to share. "In our case, I explained, we have been given the gift of reminding people about heaven and how much God loves us."

The knowing smile on Maya's cherubic face told me that she fully understood her 'mission' in this life. Looking deeply into her sky blue eyes, I knew that God had chosen well.

The following story is in Tamara's own words:

My daughter was born with a beautiful and creative imagination.

From a very young age her days were filled with endless hours of tea parties, dressing up, playing house and drawing. I was always amazed that she was so content to play alone.

At bedtime, she would tell me how much fun she had playing with her friends. Some of the names she had mentioned before but there would always be a name or two that were new. Some of the names I thought were quite creative for imaginary friends.

My little girl spent many countless hours lost in her own world with these imaginary friends. Oh, how I wanted to keep her three years old forever.

One day she was busy playing alone in her room. She was so engrossed in her conversation with her 'friends' that she didn't notice I had stopped in her doorway. It caught my attention that she would just chatter away then pause as if awaiting an answer. I watched and listened as this went on for several minutes.

"Hi, Sweetie, having fun?" I asked curiously.

"Yep, having a tea party with my friends. They're angels!" she replied.

Her face was just glowing with her big blue eyes dancing and a smile going from ear to ear.

"Oh, they are?" I asked.

She often talked about her angels, but I never associated them with her imaginary friends.

"Yep, they're telling me funny stories," she said, looking back at her teatime companions.

"OK, enjoy your party and tell your angels I said hello," I told her.

"Mom, go talk to your own," she told me, a bit protective of her new friends.

"What?" I muttered, caught a bit off guard.

"Go talk to your own, you have them all around you. Angels are everywhere," she said.

She again batted her big blue eyes at me and turned back to hand out more cookies to her teatime guests.

Because of the advice of a very wise three year old, my world changed. I learned to talk to my angels.

Several months after my first meeting with Maya, Tamara brought her son,

Chase, to see me. Contained within this young boy's nine year old body was a very wise and compassionate old soul.

What struck me most about Chase was his ability to clearly remember a lifetime in which he landed on the beaches at Normandy on D-Day. Despite growing up in a military family, Operation Overlord, wasn't something I was well versed on at the age of nine. My guess is, that most children his age and even older have very little knowledge about World War II and even less knowledge as to the specifics of uniforms worn or weapons used during the invasion.

Even more striking was the manner in which he spoke about the experiences at Normandy Beach. Sitting straight up in his chair, hands resting perfectly at his sides, I felt as thought I were talking to a seasoned military veteran In a very calm manner he began to speak in a tone far beyond his nine years. I could clearly see his facial expression change as he recounted in great detail, the sounds of bullets whizzing by his body and of mortar shells landing nearby. His voice became very serious as he told me about the smell of sulfur and the sick feelings in his stomach as he looked at the dead bodies around him.

Asking him to tell me what he saw in the area around him, he described in great detail German artillery and their positions along the beach head. Chase talked about the characteristics of German military uniforms. He also spoke about the sometimes peaceful and other times grotesque look upon the faces of the dead soldiers.

Chase was proud to have served and been a part of what happened on those beaches in 1944. Still, I could feel a sense of loss which was carried forward into this lifetime.

A look of sadness came over Chase's face, and he began to slowly nod his head. His voice became somber as he said, "I'd like to go back some day, Denise. Back to Normandy. A lot of guys stayed there. I'd like to see it all again. I just want to see it again."

Chase's dream is to graduate, like his grandfather did, from the United States Naval Academy at Annapolis. "This time around," he said, "I'd like to fly jets."

I have no doubt that Chase will fulfill his dreams of returning to Normandy and of flying Navy jets. The spirit of the warrior remains alive and well in Chase. Something tells me however, that the warrior he will become in this new millennium will fight on vastly different fronts than the warrior he once was.

Chase's mother writes:

My oldest son was terrified of thunderstorms.

If a storm arrived during the day, we would quickly move our activities to the basement to distract him.

The faintest rumble of thunder at night or the mention of storms during the evening news would ensure he would be safely tucked in bed between my husband and I for the night.

When he was about five years old, a storm rolled in around 2:00 a.m. He was still in his own bed, but I knew it wouldn't be too long before he bounded across the hall and jumped into bed with us.

The storm came and went. I was wide awake, but I wasn't sure if I was awake from the storm or in hope that he had finally learned to sleep through the thunder and lightening.

In the morning he was busy examining the back of the cereal box at breakfast.

"Did you know a storm went through last night and you slept right through it?" I said. "See, storms don't have to be scary."

"Oh, no mom. It did wake me up! When I heard the thunder I started to get up, but when I rolled over there was a face on the wall. I looked at the face and it smiled at me. I knew it was there to keep me safe. I just stayed in bed and went back to sleep.

He is now ten years old. He still doesn't like thunderstorms, but since that night, he has only wandered into our room a few times and then it was only during very bad storms.

He also still clearly recalls the face on the wall.

Perhaps it was his Guardian Angel he saw that night!

Are Guardian Angels real? Absolutely!

Each of us experiences the presence of angels in our own way and at different times in our lives.

Take a moment now to reflect upon an experience in which you felt as though you were in the company of Angels.

The times in my life when I felt the presence of Angels:

_____

_____

_____

_____

_____

_____

_____

_____

_____

_____

Meeting Your Angels

Here is an easy exercise which will help you perceive the presence of angels in their many forms and colors:

Take a moment either in the morning or evening to be still. To begin with, five minutes will do. You may increase that time when you feel ready to do so. Find a comfortable space, where you won't be disturbed and light a candle. By lighting a candle, you are creating a sacred space. The candle flame represents spirit in its purest form. You may wish to softly focus your sight on the flame as you center yourself.

Centering yourself is as easy as slowly inhaling a long breath in through your nose and down through your body, and then exhaling it slowly through your mouth. Repeating this three times balances your energy centers and prepares you for divine guidance.

After centering yourself, simply ask your Guardian Angel, or an Angel such as Michael, Gabrielle, Uriel or Raphael to speak to you.

Then, pay attention.

Pay attention to the way your body feels. Listen with your 'inner' ear to any sounds or words that may come forth. Pay attention to your third eye, or 'inner screen' as I call for any visuals that may present themselves.

Angels will let us know they are present in many different ways. You may feel a warm and tingly sensation around your body, or perhaps even a cool breeze will gently blow by. Some people report seeing a shimmering light out of the corner of their eyes. Just as they go to look at it fully, it suddenly disappears. For some people, the presence of angels is marked by the sounds of celestial tones or angelic singing which can be heard either by the inner ear, or in some cases by the outer ear.

Visually, Angels will appear to us in a way in which our 'spiritual antenna' can perceive them. Because Angels are beings of pure Light, they may come to us in the form of colorful balls of light. My clients and students report that for them, they tend to appear in orbs of purple, white, green or gold. This isn't to say that they will only appear in those colors. It's been my personal experience to see an angel in the form of a beautiful red ball of light, floating gently across my inner eye. Each will experience angels in ways that are as unique and individual as we are.

Whether you see your Angel standing before you in the form of a human with magnificent wings, or hear the celestial tones of the angelic realm in your inner ear, you can be certain that you have been in the presence of angels because of a sense of warmth and love that comes with all angelic visitations.

After inviting your Angel to come and sit with you, take a moment to record what happened, audibly, visually or physically during this exercise. If it feels as though nothing has happened, repeat the exercise each day until divine contact is made. There is no need to rush. Remember that everything happens in perfect timing.

Day 1

_____

_____

_____

_____

_____

Day 2

In addition to inviting your Angel to sit with you, ask your Angel if there is a message that it wishes to convey. Once again, pay attention to your thoughts, feelings and intuitions.

Symbols and signs are ways in which angels convey a message. You may feel a symbol, such as a dove, a rainbow or a rose. You may also see a sign such as one of these in a vision on your inner screen. Simply pay attention.

Take a moment to record the message that was given to you. Write about any signs or symbols, feelings or thoughts that crossed through your mind. How did the message make you feel?

_____

_____

_____

_____

_____

Day 3

Sit quietly once again today, light a candle and invite your Angel to sit with you. By doing this exercise three days in a row, you may now begin to feel the familiar presence of your angel as you prepare your sacred space. The more you invite your angels(s) to be part of your daily life, the more acquainted you will become with their energy.

Once again, ask your Angel if there is a message or a sign they wish to share with you. On this day, begin paying attention to those signs as they manifest in your physical world. When I ask Metatron to be present with me, I will invariably experience a beautiful rainbow or a lovely white dove during the course of my day.

Don't limit yourself as to how the sign will appear. Whether I am greeted by a heavenly rainbow in the sky, a rendition of "Somewhere Over the Rainbow" on the radio or a rainbow bumper sticker on the car in front of me, I know that Metatron is reminding me of something that I already know. I am never, ever alone.

What sign(s) has your Angel shared with you. How did they manifest during your day?

_____

_____

_____

_____

_____

_____

_____

Sometimes I am asked, "Denise, why would someone want to know if they have an Angel in their life? Why would someone want to see a sign from an Angel if they did have one?"

My answer is quite simple.

Speaking from personal experience, there have been times in my life when knowing that I was in the company of an angel, saved me from feeling very alone. I believe we all have those times. They are part of our life journey.

Sometimes, our faith is shaken or shattered.

To know that beyond our three dimensional physical reality, that there is a messenger from God who accompanies us on our journey, who shares our joys and our sorrows is sometimes all we need to help get us through.

"Knock and the door shall be opened."

Perhaps there is a magnificent Light Being from Heaven waiting for us to simply ring the doorbell.

Aside from lifting us up spiritually, Angels love to be part of celebrations such as anniversaries, weddings, birthdays and bar mitzvah's. When planning such a sacred event, invite the Angels to partake in the planning. You'll be amazed at how smoothly things fall into place. Remember to invite them to the party. Your guests will have a wonderful time celebrating in the company of angels. Don't be surprised when your guests tell you that they've had the best time that they can remember in a very long time.

The Animal Kingdom

The idea of animals as spirit guides is part of nearly all indigenous cultures around the globe. According to many ancient spiritual traditions, each of us is accompanied by members of the animal kingdom as we walk our sacred path.

These animals, sometimes known as totems or familiars, represent a part of our spirit that lies deep within us. They are a connection to our Maker.

My ceremonial or spiritual name is Dana RavenWolf. I have been so named because of the totem company I keep.

The Raven, Wolf and Siberian Tiger are my totem animals.

Raven represents the mysteries of Spirit. She travels 'into the darkness to retrieve the Light'. Raven is my companion as I travel into the Realm of Spirit. She represents that part of my soul that has the ability to travel beyond physical time and space. As I grow spiritually, she helps me uncover and understand the greater mysteries.

Each morning on my way to work, Raven greets me. Soaring high above me in the air, or looking at me from alongside the road, she reminds me to follow my true soul path. Her shiny, onyx colored wings inspire my heart to fly above the ordinary, into the extraordinary.

Wolf, the teacher, is also a protector. My fierce sentinel keeps a watchful eye on me and my surroundings. Whether I am traveling the spiritual realms, or participating in sacred ceremony on the earth plane, Wolf encircles the perimeter of the location, marking his territory and creating a circle of protection for me. A ferocious growl, and fangs revealed, warn me of imminent danger fast approaching. Wolf engages in battle on my behalf, warding off any would be menace on the spiritual plane.

When my spirit is feeling low, he also provides a soft, furry neck to hug and a warm nose to rub against my own.

Tiger reminds me to be courageous as I walk my earth journey. He helps me to face my fears, and teaches me to move through them with grace. His lithe body and elegant gate represent sensuality. Living a life filled with passion and daring is Tiger's message to me.

I keep Tiger with me at the office in the form of a tiger-eye carving. I also keep Tiger with me in the form of a bracelet that I had created. The bracelet, which is made of tiger eye, garnet, crystal and jasper exudes the energy of Tiger.

Once in a while, a different Totem animal will step in to deliver a brief, but important message.

Bear for instance, steps in on occasion to remind me to slow down and go within. During a week filled with frenzied activities, he came to me in my dream time with a very poignant message.

In my dream, I found myself climbing a stairway. Bear was in front of me. Not moving quickly enough for my liking, I kept pushing on him to get him to move faster. After the third shove on his furry black behind, he slowly turned around and bit me on my right leg.

Horrified, I could feel his teeth sinking deeply into my flesh. A stream of crimson colored blood poured from the puncture wounds and onto the cement. It formed a pool around my feet.

Looking straight into the bears' eyes, I asked, "Why on earth did you do this to me?"

In a voice that reminded me of Papa Bear in the story of Goldilocks, he replied, "Because, I could get your attention no other way. You must slow down."

At that moment, the blood, the wounds, and the searing pain disappeared.

Let's just say, Bear's message was clearly understood and I took it easy for the next several days. All activities that were not absolutely required of me, were cancelled. Only those activities that brought joy and relaxation took place.

Have you ever wondered why you've always been attracted to a particular animal such as a hawk? Does hawk often show up at an important occasion in your life or when you feel you need guidance? This Totem Animal is harbinger of many important messages. Hawk represents flight and freedom. He speaks to you of seeing clearly and soaring to new heights. Hawk reminds you of your infinite potential to rise above the mundane and sail among the stars. He is a sign that anything is possible.

Hawk is also a protector.

Years ago my family lived in a home adjacent to our church. When my son was four years old he asked me if he could ride across the church parking lot on his new bike all by himself. As I thought about my son and his quest for the freedom that comes with a new bike, a beautiful brown hawk rose up from the woods behind the church and perched on the phone line directly above us.

Knowing that Hawk would protect him, I agreed to let Dane make the grand journey from our driveway to the other side of the church lot. As my little adventurer began to pedal away, the regal hawk took leave of the phone wire and flew directly above him until they both came to rest at the opposite end of the church property.

After waving to me and giving me the triumphant thumbs up sign, Dane and his hawk companion made the journey home. As hawk again perched on the phone wire above our heads, I thanked him for protecting and guiding my little man.

To this day, hawk shows up in Dane's life as a positive confirmation and reminder of his unlimited potential.

How do you 'call in' your own Totem Animal? It's quite easy.

Just as you would with any other sacred ceremony, create a reverent space and become comfortable. Take a moment to thank your Teachers and Guides for being with you as you perform this ancient practice.

After sitting for a moment in silence and in the loving embrace of your Spiritual Guides, close your eyes and ask your Animal Totem to please come forward. You can do this right out loud if you wish.

And then wait.

If you are outdoors or near a window, you may very well see your Totem walk, run, crawl or fly directly up to or near you.

With your eyes closed you may begin to see your Totem Animal with your third eye.

If you are clairsentient, you may feel your totem animal or you may hear it. Simply pay attention to your surroundings and to the information that your body receives.

You may be quite surprised to find out who your Totem is, or perhaps you've always known and this will be confirmation.

Once your ceremony is complete, thank your Totem for walking the journey of spirit with you.

My Totem Animal is: _____

What my Totem Animal represents to me:

_____

_____

_____

_____

There are many wonderful books regarding Totem Animals. One of my favorites is "Animal Speak", by Ted Andrews.

The following meditation from my CD, "Beyond the Veil Lies a Mystic Journey," will help you bring forth your totem animal guide:

The Totem Call

Breathe deeply and gently close your eyes.

Exhale and relax your entire body.

Breathe deeply once again and as you exhale, relax your mind.

Breathe deeply once more and as you exhale, settle comfortably into your surroundings.

Find yourself in a forest clearing.

It is early evening and you are sitting alongside a warm crackling fire.

You are comfortable here.

As the sun slowly fades from view the evening sky becomes indigo.

Brilliant stars of far off solar systems light the night sky. Watch as they twinkle and dance in the heavens above you.

Breathe in this wondrous site and enjoy.

As you prepare for sacred ceremony you invite the guardians of the North, the South, the West, and the East, above and below to join you. Feel them enter your sacred space.

It is time now to offer sweet grass, sage and cedar to the keepers of the earth, wind, fire and water. As you place these offerings in the fire, feel the spirits of nature join in this blessed event.

Calling upon the four leggeds, those with wings and those of the water you can see something awaken within the fire and within the starlit air.

Gazing upon the flames burning bright orange, yellow and blue you can feel your totem animal begin to emerge. Beckon it forth.

Watch, feel and listen as your animal totem makes its presence known to you.

Thank your totem for agreeing to walk the path of spirit with you.

Pay attention as your totem now speaks to you in words, sounds, images, thoughts and feelings.

Take a moment to thank the Creator for the Gift of this sacred journey called life and for the gift of your companion in Spirit.

Take time to thank the guardians and keepers for their presence on this night.

Now bring your attention back to your physical body and back to the sounds in the room. And when you are ready, very gently open your eyes.

Spend a moment recording your experience calling in your Totem Animal.

Faeries

A sub-group of the Angelic Realm, these nature spirits inhabit and oversee the goings on in our gardens, our forests, and all places where nature exists. They also step into our lives to remind us to play. One must remember to call upon the Over lighting Diva of the Fae Kingdom, Pan, when these mischievous light beings get rambunctious!

My first experience with the Faerie Kingdom came in the winter of 2000. It was during the evening in the dead of winter that the furnace in my new home decided to go out. My simple solution to the cold was to take a hot lavender bubble bath.

As I was soaking in the bathtub, I became aware of two tiny figures standing on the edge of my tub. At first I chuckled to myself because I was convinced that I had truly gone over the edge! However, rather than just dismiss the wee folk as a figment of my imagination, I asked them their names and asked them to give me a sign that they were indeed real.

All of a sudden, there came a loud "boom" as the furnace, which had been out for hours, came back to life. With heat now pouring out of the bathroom vents, I watched with much delight as Jonathan and Rebecca pointed at me with their delicate little hands and laughed out loud. When they were finished laughing at the dumbfounded expression on my face, they proceeded to tell me why they had appeared at all:

"Denise, we represent the faeries who reside in your garden during the Spring and Summer and Autumn months. We wish to know if it would be possible for us to dwell in your home during the Winter. With the arrival of each Spring, we will once again reside in your garden."

To which I responded, "Of course you may."

And with a very hardy "Thank you, Denise." Jonathan and Rebecca faded from view.

Having a very limited knowledge of the workings of the Faerie Realm, I was unaware that along with my response, I should have included a clause about Faerie behavior in my home.

Before I knew it, articles of clothing were coming up missing. Clothing with shiny things, like belt buckles, beadwork or glitter. The Christmas tree in the family room was found sprawled upon the floor with colored bulbs strewn about, yet the tree skirt had been neatly tucked and folded around the base!

The final straw as they say came the day that I received a very harried phone call from my mother:

"Hello, Denise, this is your mother."

"Hello, Mother," I replied.

My mother said, "Denise, something very strange is going on inside your house right now. There is music playing. Beautiful music playing everywhere. But, I can't find where it's coming from."

I responded, "It's the Faeries Mother."

"It's the what?" she replied.

I said, "The Faeries."

"Are you kidding me? Faeries?" asked my bewildered mother.

To which I replied, "Yes, Mother, Faeries."

"Well, I don't believe in Faeries." she countered.

I warned her, "Don't say that out loud, Mom."

"Why?" she inquired.

"Because you'll upset them," I cautioned.

"I don't believe we're having this conversation," she replied.

"Believe it, Mom," I said.

"This is just crazy! You've got music playing in your home, and I don't know where it's coming from. And now you tell me it's Faeries?" replied my disbelieving mother.

"Yes, Mom, that's what I'm telling you," I answered.

"I still don't believe it," she said.

"Mom, don't say that anymore. They'll hear you," I whispered.

"Denise, I'm going to lunch with Joyce. I'll call you when I get home," she said.

I responded, "Okay, Mom. Just don't say anything else out loud about not believing in the Wee Folk, okay?"

"I'll call you when I get back from lunch with Joyce," she said.

Two hours later I received the following phone call:

"Denise, this is your mother."

"Hello, Mother. How was lunch?" I asked.

"You're not going to believe this," she responded.

"Not going to believe what?" I inquired.

"When I got home from lunch with Joyce, I walked into your house and found all of the kitchen curtains on the floor," she replied.

I said, "Mother, I told you not to make fun of the Faeries."

A long period of silence followed…and then she spoke.

"Yes you did. You know, I'm used to unusual things happening around you, but I wouldn't have dreamed in a million years that Faeries were real." was her response.

"Do you believe it now?" I asked.

"Yes. Now what?" she replied.

I answered with, "Apologize to the Faeries and ask them to please behave themselves from now on."

My mother then whispered, "Okay, but I still can't believe this happened. This is scary and amazing all at the same time!"

To which I replied "Don't be scared Mom. Just think of them as itty bitty angels with an attitude!"

After my mother's rather dramatic indoctrination to the world of the Faerie Folk, I had a serious conversation with their over lighting Deva, Pan. I asked Pan to please keep my house faeries under control until Spring came. I then proceeded to inform my resident wee folk that if they didn't behave themselves, I would be serving their eviction notice, post haste. After all, I couldn't have them scaring my mother at every turn and replacing the Christmas ornaments was getting expensive!

Over the past few years, we've come to a very comfortable living arrangement with them out in the Faerie Garden during the warm months and inside our home during winter. While on occasion we still find ourselves searching for 'lost' shiny objects, we've learned that the Faeries are always willing to return them when we ask nicely.

Mother Nature

In Her infinite wisdom, Mother Nature provides us with spiritual insight along the Mystic Journey. She often provides us with a reflection of our own lives. At times, phrases such as, "My life is like a whirlwind," "She has a sunny outlook," or "Still waters run deep," are used to describe ourselves and others.

The energy of Mother Moon, Father Sun, Brother Wind and Sister Stars affects the rhythm of our own human body. The stages of our life are referred to as seasons.

As with all living things, if you ask Mother Nature for a sign, She will undoubtedly oblige your request. To hear Her answer, you must pay very close attention.

As an exercise in this form of communication, take time on a starry night to ask Mother Nature for a sign that you are connected to and supported by Universal Grace. Then pay close attention to the formation of the clouds, the wind, the planets and the stars. You'll be amazed by Her response. While you may not hear Her speak to you in a conventional manner, She will most definitely speak to you in a manner that your Spirit understands.

To the Native Americans, Grandfather Stone is very much alive and full of wisdom. Have you ever been out in nature and come upon a stone that appeared to have a face on it?

I have.

Looking into the face of Grandfather Stone always makes me smile. When I place my hand upon his surface and listen with my ears, my eyes and my heart, He always tells me a story that my soul needs to hear.

Sometimes, Grandfather Stone wears a message for us on His sleeve.

Within the cool, moist sand of Merlin's Cave in Cornwall, England, my friend Teri discovered a large, dark gray stone with ivory markings that were clearly meant as a message for us.

Moments before her discovery, we had been participating in a prayer circle dedicated to world peace. The songs being sung by our group of 22, filled the cave and spilled out upon the beach. The cave echoed with our petitions for global harmony, drawing onlookers who had become mesmerized by the tranquil energy we had created.

By the time we finished our ceremony, a small crowd of people had gathered at the mouth of the cave, which is located under the ruins of what many say are the remains of King Arthur's castle. Many of them thanked us for our praying for world peace. Others simply smiled, clearly touched by what they had witnessed.

Someone from our group remarked that it would be really cool to find King Arthur's sword, Excalibur, in the cave named for his magical consort, Merlin.

As those words left our companions lips, Teri found the dark grey stone. Embedded in its rough, craggy surface was an 8 inch ivory marking clearly in the shape of a sword!

There was no mistaking the sword, or the message it was intended to deliver to our group.

Excalibur represents the wielding of Truth. It represents Arthur's kingdom of Camelot where peace and equality prevailed.

It was Excalibur that accompanied Arthur to the Round Table, where the 12 Knights and 12 Ladies of the Realm were considered wholly equal.

Some messages are timeless.

On that day, in Merlin's Cave, Mother Nature provided us with a reminder of the need for truth, and equality in the search for global peace. She even went as far as to etch it in stone!

When we look at the healing properties of stone energies, flower essences or herbal remedies, we begin to understand that our Earth Mother has truly provided for our every need as only She can.

Giving our Spirit respite and rejuvenation is one of Her greatest gifts. If we're willing to take the time to stop and smell the roses, that is.

One of my favorite exercises to help us connect with Mother Nature involves sitting under a tree.

With your back resting comfortably against its trunk, become aware of the energy moving along the length of your spine. As you continue to connect with the Spirit of the Tree, ask it to tell you a story or to give you a message from the Creator.

Pay attention to your psychic senses. A message will arrive in the form of a vision, a feeling, or a verbal communication that you can hear with your inner ear. If you're lucky, Mother Nature may whisper to you in the wind that moves through the leaves that crown your tree.

My message from the Tree Spirit:

_____

_____

_____

"If you could get rid of yourself just once, the secret of secrets would open to you. The face of the unknown, hidden beyond the universe would appear on the mirror of your perception."

Jalaluddin Rumi (1207—1273), Sufi mystic and poet

Crystal Balls & Other Cool Tools for Accessing Heavenly Direction

hat follows are very brief explanations of the tools most commonly used to divine information from Spirit.

Tarot

Many believe that the origin of these cards belongs to the Knights Templar, while others believe that the origin of this oracle dates back many centuries prior to this Knightly Order. Some look to the Rosicrucian's and the Cathars as the developers of this widely practiced divining system.

Regardless of where they began, Tarot is a very useful tool for gaining insight into a situation, or for taking a look at future possibilities.

Go to almost any bookstore these days and you will find dozens of beautifully illustrated Tarot decks. While some still use the standard 78 card deck with multiple reading layouts, other oracle decks are quite simple to use and require no formal layouts. You will know which deck is right for you when you pick it up. The cards will simply 'feel right' to you.

Oracle cards are an offshoot of Tarot, that typically contain a deck of 44 cards with very brief and specific messages on them.

I think of them as greeting cards from the Universe.

Each morning I ask Spirit to help me draw a card that contains a message I need to see that day. Throughout the day, I reflect upon that message and at night, I marvel at how relevant it was to my overall experience.

Pendulum

Whether you are using a favorite necklace, or a specially designed pendulum made of crystals, stone or metal, these divining tools put you in immediate contact with the voice of your higher self and of your guides. By programming your pendulum to give you a yes, no or even a 'mind your own business' response to your questions, you will receive a quick, no nonsense answer to questions ranging from the mundane to the extraordinary.

You will know which pendulum is right for you when you pick it up and hold it. If it begins to vibrate in your hand, or swing back and forth or in circles when you hold it, you know this pendulum is 'calling your name'.

Once you have chosen your pendulum, or it has chosen you, it is a good idea to cleanse it by smudging it with incense or running it under cool water to rid it of energies not your own. It is important then to wear it on your person for a few days so that it synchronizes with your personal energy.

After you do this, it is important not to let others touch your pendulum, as this will interfere with the resonance that you have created with it. If someone does come in contact with your pendulum, simply smudge it once again with some sandalwood, copal or frankincense incense or depending on what it is made of, you can also run it under cool water. Putting it outside in the rays of the sun or the full moon also restores its balance.

Once your pendulum has been cleansed and synchronized with your personal energy, it is time to program it. While holding your pendulum steady by its chain or string, ask your angels and guides to show you a yes response. Watch how your pendulum begins to move. This is the manner in which your guides will give you a positive response. Steady your pendulum once again and ask your guides and angels to show you a 'no' response. As before, watch how your pendulum begins to move. This reflects a negative response. Repeat this process to see a 'mind your own business' or any other type of response you might like to program.

You may also tell your guides how you would like a yes or no response to be delivered. Typically, a horizontal or vertical swing is requested. At other times a clockwise or counterclockwise movement is asked for. It's completely up to you and your guides as to how you will program your own personal pendulum answer code.

Runes

This age old Celtic divination system is typically made up of a set of small highly polished stones that are engraved with sacred Celtic symbols. You can get them in most any stone that you desire. From clear quartz to hematite, use your intuition as to which type of stone feels best to you. You may even purchase a set of wooden runes if you feel compelled to work with the spirit of wood.

As with tarot, you can use the simple method of asking a question and choosing only one rune stone for an answer, or you can use one of several elaborate reading layouts that will be included in the Book of Runes that accompanies your set of Celtic divination stones.

A great way to connect with the wisdom of the Runes is to create your own set of Rune stones. You may purchase the Book of Runes separately and collect your own stones from special places you may have visited or from a sacred spot that you enjoy spending time in. Ask each of your specially chosen stones to tell you which Celtic symbol they would enjoy having etched or painted on their surface. If you listen very closely, you will hear their answers!

I-Ching

These Eastern divination tools are ancient in origin. You will find them in sets of round brass coins, flat wooden sticks from 5 to 12 inches long, or even as four sided plastic pieces that look like miniature two by fours. Both the coins and the sticks are etched with lines that are placed in specific formation.

By tossing the coins or sticks and then 'reading' their line patterns, you will be given divine guidance. Each set of I-Ching coins or sticks comes with a book or a deck of cards which will help you decipher the meaning of the lines and patterns.

Scrying with Crystal Balls and Mirrors

Perhaps the most famous of all psychic divining techniques is known as scrying. Whether using a clear crystal ball, a mirror or a quartz crystal, this form of psychic work involves using a focal point for your eyes to gently concentrate and gaze upon so that your mind can become free of outside interference and internal 'noise'.

While many actually see visions within the crystal or mirror, others are able to feel, or hear guidance. Because their eyes are focused on an object, the voice of their Higher Self and of their guides is able to come through an uncluttered mind.

Psychometry

Every time we touch an object, we leave behind an energetic imprint. Because the things we touch come to exude our own personal energy, through psychometry, we are able to read this imprint.

By holding an object such as a wrist watch or a ring we can sense the energy that has been left behind by a person. Through our psychic senses we can listen to the history of the object and the history of those who have owned it.

Take for instance, the beautiful gold ring that I purchased in 2003 in Palm Springs, CA.

During the course of teaching a Mystic Journey workshop, I invited everyone in the class to hold my ring and feel what it had to tell them. Without giving them the history of my ring, I then asked my students to tell me in one or two words the feelings they had while holding it. They used the following words to express what they felt:

Laughter, warmth, sunny, female, ocean, sand, love, heart, hot, affection, canyon, rock.

Delighted with their efforts, I told them the story of how I traveled to Palm Springs with a dear friend to spend four days with a mutual friend of ours. Whenever the three of us are together, an adventure always ensues. Our days in California were filled with shopping, eating, sunning, hiking, meditation and always: laughter.

One morning we decided to spend time meditating and hiking in a mystical place called Palm Canyon. This site is especially sacred to the Native American people in California.

On this particular day, the morning air was crisp and the sky breathtakingly beautiful. It appeared as though Spirit had used the sky as a canvas to paint a sea of orange, gold, magenta and blue. It was a scene unlike anything we had ever witnessed before.

As the three of us sat on the rim of the canyon we quietly listened to the voice of spirit speaking to us from deep within the canyon walls. Directly across from us, we watched as the face of Spirit manifested itself in the form of a gigantic sculpture of a Native American man protruding from the side of the canyon. He seemed to be crying out to us in a language long forgotten. It was as though he was asking us to help him call the Spirits of Nature back to Palm Canyon, back to Mother Earth. With suburbs growing up around this sacred place, it felt as though he were speaking to us in desperation, reminding us all of the wisdom of the Old Ways. It was something the three of us agreed we would never forget.

We left the canyon knowing that we had experienced the Spirit of The Elements speaking directly to us. I knew that I wanted a reminder of my time in Palm Canyon. I found that reminder in the gold ring that I purchased later that day.

It was the texture of the ring that reminded me of the canyon walls. The three diamonds on top reminded me of the three of us, and the gold itself spoke to me of the divine message we each received in the canyon that morning.

The memory of that day comes flooding back to me whenever I wear my Canyon ring, as I've now come to call it. And when others hold my little golden treasure, it speaks to them of the memory that it holds for me. It comes in the form of words like laughter, warmth, sunny, female, ocean, sand, love, heart, hot, affection, canyon and rock.

Being a Channel for the Voice of Spirit

his form of divination is perhaps the least understood. While some people have come to believe that a channeler opens himself/herself up to be taken over by evil entities, quite the opposite is true.

Channelers simply 'tune in' to the voice of the Divine. They listen to messages from Spirit and then share them in written or spoken form. If you have read Neale Donald Walsch's, "Conversations with God" series, or Lee Carroll's, "Kryon" series, you have read some of the most valuable channeled information of our time.

Different Forms of Channeling

Light Trance Channeling – The channeler is fully aware of spirit and what is being said. Through, clairsentience, clairaudience and clairvoyance the channeler 'listens' to the voice of their guide(s).

Deep Trance Channeling – The channeler is in a state of unconsciousness and allows Spirit to 'step into' their body, to be used as a vehicle for spiritual communication.

Independent Writing – A form of channeling in which the written word is done entirely by Spirit using the channeler's hand.

Automatic or Inspired Writing – Similar to channeling, automatic or inspired writing is a matter of holding a pen or pencil and asking for guidance. As guidance comes through audibly, visually or through physical sensation, you write all that you hear, see or feel. Do not edit your writing; just let it flow through your chakra system and out through your pen. Once you are finished writing and begin to read what you have written, you will be amazed at the divine guidance you were able to access!

In all forms of channeling, the channeler is always in control of the situation and has the ability to start and stop the channeling at any time.

After creating a warm, sacred space, spend a quiet moment asking Spirit to speak to you through channeled writing. You may ask a specific question that you would like Spirit to give you insight to, or simply ask what it is Spirit would like you to know at this moment in time.

When you feel inspired to write, begin doing so:

Writing a love letter to your Higher Self and listening with your Heart for the answer is another fun way to channel divinely inspired messages. Take a moment to think about something that your Heart yearns for and write it below.

Dear Higher Self,

My Heart is longing to:

_____

_____

_____

_____

_____

_____

_____

_____

_____

_____

_____

_____

_____

After you have finished writing your heart's desire, take a moment to state out loud or in silence what you have just written.

Then quietly listen to the answer as it is given to you by your Soul.

The answer may come in feelings, thoughts, or symbols. It may even come in musical form or a knowingness. The important thing is to take note of everything that you sense and record it below:

Dear Child of the Light,

Your first step in fulfilling this longing is to:

_____

_____

_____

_____

_____

_____

How will you integrate this information into your life to help you reach your goal?

_____

_____

_____

_____

_____

_____

_____

"It is a terrible thing to see and have no vision."

Helen Keller, (1880—1968), American memoirist,
who lectured widely on behalf of sightless people.

There is No Such Thing as a Coincidence.
a.k.a. Watching for Signs Along the Road of Life

igns and symbols are a universal form of communication. Many times, when we work with our Angels, Teachers and Guides, they speak to us in this manner.

Spirit often uses signs as a way of giving us direction when we are lost and looking for guidance. As the occupants of the driver's seat during our earthly journey, it is up to us to take notice of the signs and to act accordingly.

Often times, we ask God for a sign that we are on the right path. And even though the signs are clearly given, we sometimes lack the courage to follow through.

I compare it to driving along an interstate highway headed for a day long adventure.

157

You know precisely where you want to go, but aren't exactly sure how to get there.

Even with a detailed map in hand, complete with exit information, we sometimes second guess the directions and fail to take the right exit. Having driven completely past our departure point, we suddenly realize that our vehicle is now headed in the wrong direction.

After driving much farther than was initially necessary, we exit at the nearest highway off ramp. With great frustration, we turn our vehicle right back around, and head in the opposite direction. All of those extra gyrations just to get us to where we were supposed to be in the first place.

Those are the moments when I want to kick myself squarely in the rear end and tell myself, "Way to go Denise. If you would have paid attention to the signs, everything would have gone a whole lot smoother. You wouldn't be in the fix you're now in. Nice job."

This situation can be applied to many other instances in our lives when we didn't listen to the voice of the Divine.

Since each of us is a unique, one-of-a-kind Spirit having a human experience, each individual will perceive and understand symbolic messages from our guides and angels in a different manner. Think of symbols as a special communication code between you and your guides. Don't be afraid to ask your guides to work with you in setting up your own special symbolic meanings.

Sometime signs and symbols are given in a very entertaining way. Following is an example of this, as recounted by my dear friend, Darlene:

Dear Denise,

Through our many adventures together over the years, and experiencing numerous 'coincidences' that were not coincidences, there are way too many stories to put into words. However, I believe this story is one definitely worth committing to paper.

You always tell me that I overanalyze everything and have to get signs that are "in my face" so I know where the sign is coming from. I thought I would share this one amazing experience. I don't think it gets much more "in your face" than this.

During our recent trip to Palm Desert in March 2005, as we were tanning by the pool early in the morning, I shared with you that is seemed as though in my life, for various reasons, I felt like I was in the middle of a tornado, and was not sure where I was going to land.

In your usual helpful response, you told me to just stay centered in the middle of the storm and everything would work out the way it is supposed to. "Just think of it like the Wizard of Oz," you said. "There are lessons to be learned and trials and tribulations to experience before it all makes sense."

Then as we were preparing to go out and about for the day, you asked my guides that I be given a sign in the form of something related to the Wizard of Oz. This would be my confirmation that everything was happening just as it should, and that ultimately my current experiences were happening for my greatest good.

One of my all time favorite songs is "Somewhere Over the Rainbow/What a Wonderful World" by the late Hawaiian sing/songwriter, Israel Kamakawiwo'ole, better known as "IZ".

As we shopped in a candle store in Palm Springs later that day, you decided to go into a small CD store next door because you wanted to get IZ's "Facing Future" CD and you just knew they would have it. Of course, they did.

We continued eating out and shopping for the remainder of the day until it was time to head back to the condo. On the way back, sitting quietly in the back seat of the car, I began to think about our conversation at the pool that morning. I had not yet received a sign with regard to the Wizard of Oz. While waiting for the red light to turn green at the next intersection, (which, by the way, takes so long to happen in Palm Springs that one could atrophy while waiting), I thought about the Wizard of Oz sign that I was supposed to be watching for.

I began to look out the window into the darkened sky for my sign. It was at this busy intersection, that you indicated you were going to open your new CD and put it in to the player. After unwrapping your CD, you handed me the CD case and said, "Well, Darlene, here's your sign." Inside the CD jacket were the words, "The Wizard of Oz and the Man of Steele."

We listened to the soothing Hawaiian music and the angelic voice of IZ, until we reached our destination. After a long day of shopping, we felt a sit in the hot tub was in order to soothe our tired feet.

Sitting in the hot tub under a crystal clear azure sky and gazing at the stars, you told me I would continue to receive signs in the form of things relating to the Wizard of Oz, but in addition to this I would receive rainbows, as a constant reminder that everything would be well in my life. While that may not seem like an unusual sign to receive, it all came together for me when we came back to Michigan.

We got back late on a Sunday evening, and the following Friday afternoon I had an appointment with a prospective client. As I got out of my car and went up to the door, the welcome mat at the front door had the ruby slippers with the saying "There's no place like home" written on it. I immediately thanked the Universe, and as I went to press the doorbell, I was greeted by a vinyl sticker on the window of the door , which contained a photo of all of the characters of the Wizard of Oz.

As if that weren't enough, when I walked in the front door and looked into the living room, there was a pillow on the couch with the face of the Tin Man and the saying "If I only had a heart" stitched upon it. I began smiling. Oh, and by the way, I was meeting with a husband and wife, and the wife's name was Dorothy.

As we went to their kitchen table and I sat down, I looked up at their china cabinet and it was literally packed full of Wizard of Oz figurines. But that wasn't all.

The pattern on the wallpaper in the kitchen was rainbows, and Dorothy was wearing a necklace made of dichroic glass squares in the colors of the rainbow.

During small talk with this lovely couple, Dorothy told me that her husband couldn't remember my name and she told him the way she remembered who was coming over was the fact that the neighbor on the one side of their house was her dear friend "Darlene", and on the other side of their house, the neighbors were the "Frederick's."

What a wonderful start to the weekend!

Thank you for the gifts you share with people, and all you do for me.

Blessings,
Darlene Frederick

160

*"In every truth I tell you, whoever has faith in me will do
what I am doing; indeed will do greater things still."*

Jesus the Christ (1st century of this era), Teacher and prophet
whose life and teachings form the basis of Christianity.

Sacred Sound, Making a Joyful Noise, Even in the Silence ... Shhh

Prayer

ending loving thoughts; keeping a Gratitude Journal; reciting the rosary; mindful meditation; lovingly sewing a button on a shirt. All of these are a form of prayer.

And each one of them is far more powerful than we could ever imagine.

Like raindrops to a thirsty flower, prayer fills us with loving energy and rejuvenates our Spirit. And, like a raindrop falling on a still pond, its healing effects ripple outward infinitely.

At times when we feel we have nothing to offer someone in the way of comfort, we often ask "What can I do to help?" The answer sounds so simple, and yet in times of distress it is probably the most sought after thing in the Universe. The answer is "Prayer."

Prayer comes from one of the most mighty energy centers in the Universe, the heart. When a thought or gesture is done from the heart, it sends forward an immensely powerful intention that is surrounded with love. One single person sending a prayer to the Creator on behalf of themselves or others creates a shift of such magnitude; we cannot begin to conceive of it. And even when our prayers are not answered in exactly the same manner we had intended, we can be assured that they will indeed be answered in a way that will serve our greatest and highest good.

Recently, medical studies have tested the recovery period for patients who have been prayed for, versus those who have not. The overwhelming results have been speedier recovery times, and in some cases recoveries that are nothing short of a miracle.

The healing energy of a prayer, is first received in our heart center. Its loving intention fills us with love and Light. From there it radiates outward to our entire aura, balancing our energy centers and lifting us up spiritually and physically. We radiate in the Spirit, when we are full of love. And when we radiate love, we attract love in return.

Many times when I am doing a reading for someone, I receive a message from a loved one on the other side, that the prayers that have been sent to them have been heard and received, but more than that, the prayers have been "felt." On more than one occasion, it has been described to me as a "warm, blue energy" that feels like an embrace. It has even been described to me as a warm fuzzy sweater.

Just as prayer has an uplifting effect on those of us on the physical plane, so too does it have an uplifting effect on those in Spirit.

Whether it is one solitary voice, or the voices of a multitude, prayer is a means by which change can be effected locally and globally. So, while you are at home visualizing the entire world basking in a healing pink embrace, rest assured that your healing prayer in indeed being felt in places you've never dreamed of going and by people you may never meet...in this lifetime anyway.

Take a moment to write your own special prayer:

_____

_____

_____

Positive Affirmations

When was the last time you said "I love you," and meant it? To yourself, that is!

A positive affirmation a day keeps the gloomies away. They also help to break through old thought patters that we've kept stored away in our library of outdated belief systems. Reciting a personal mantra each morning is also a great way to set the tone for the day ahead. There are several ways of doing this, and each one of them works wonders.

The Note on the Bathroom Mirror Technique:

Write your favorite affirmation(s) on a slip of paper and stick it to the bathroom mirror. This way you will see it each morning as you brush your teeth and comb your hair. Recite the mantra to yourself three consecutive times each day.

Some positive affirmations might be:

"I am perfect in the eyes of God."

"I love me just the way I am."

"I am a unique expression of the divine."

"Every day is a new opportunity to begin again."

Write your own positive affirmations:

1. _____

2. _____

3. _____

4. _____

5. _____

6. _____

A Box of Positive Intentions

Create your own affirmation box and fill it with slips of paper containing your favorite positive intentions and spiritual quotes. Each morning draw one affirmation at random and recite it three times. You can purchase a fancy gift box in a store or dress up an old shoe box with photos, beads, and glitter! Remember to be your Creative Self when you design your box. Ask your angels to help. They love to be creative!

Some positive intentions might be:

"Today I will feed my body only healthy foods and drinks."

"My Angels and Guides are my constant companions."

"Today is the first day of the rest of my life. I will let this day be
a beautiful new beginning."

"I have nothing to fear, but fear itself."

"I see the reflection of the Creator in everyone I meet."

Take a moment to write down your own special intentions and favorite quotes:

1. _____

2. _____

3. _____

4. _____

5. _____

6. _____

Gratitude List

The quickest way to bring more love and abundance into your life is by offering gratitude for the love and abundance that currently exists in your life.

Make a list of the things you are grateful for. These could be the names of special people in your life, the positive qualities that you possess, the things you have, or the wonderful things that you have done in your life. Post this list on your refrigerator, your bathroom mirror or any other place where you will see it often. The Gratitude List is a wonderful reminder of the good fortune that you have in your life.

Recite your list each day, out loud, giving thanks for everyone and every thing written on it.

I am grateful for:

1. _____

2. _____

3. _____

4. _____

5. _____

The Wisdom Wall

Both of my children have a positive affirmation mantra hanging on the wall next to their bedroom door. I created these mantras, added computer graphics and had them laminated. Each day before going to school or going to bed at night, they recite their personal mantra. Here is an example:

I AM Beautiful and Happy.

I AM Creative and Kind.

I AM the Best Student I can Be.

I AM the Best Sister I can Be.

I AM the Best Daughter I can Be.

I AM LOVED.

I AM LOVE!

Here are some positive affirmations you may wish to use:

The Light of the Creator Shines in Me and Through Me. I AM a reflection of Love.

I Release the Negativity of the Past to Live Fully Present in the Now. Now is all there is.

I AM a Child of the Light. I Live in the Light. I AM the Light.

I AM Peaceful. My Life Flows with Ease.

I AM Creative. I AM Creating a Life of Love and Abundance.

I AM Strong and Healthy. My Body is the Temple of My Spirit.

I Radiate Love and I Receive Love in Return.

I Listen to the Voice of My Higher Self and Welcome the Wisdom from Within.

Take a moment to make a list of positive affirmations of your choosing:

_____

_____

_____

_____

_____

_____

Toning

Ancestral sound and vibration is another link to our heavenly home. Ancient drumming and toning lift the energy frequency of our physical body and mind as well as our spiritual body and mind. As we raise the energy around us and through us, we are able to tap into the higher realms of existence. We are also able to bring the higher realms to us and tap into the memory of them within us.

Many of us have heard Gregorian and Buddhist Chant or Native American Drumming. Perhaps you have used a Tibetan Singing Bowl to clear a room of negative energy or a tuning fork to balance your chakras. The sacred sounds that these energy tools create move us. They stir a part of our soul that can identify with the energy that these sounds create. These techniques help us remember our wholeness, and help us to heal.

Following are some toning techniques that you will find useful in your every day life.

To begin toning, sit upright. No need to be rigid, but it is important that you be properly aligned for proper air and energy flow. Tip your chin slightly downward and part your lips, just slightly.

OM: Sanskrit word for "God," "Creator," "Allah," and "All That Is"

Toning this word (pronounced ŌM) balances and energizes the chakra system. It will also rid a room of unwanted energies and restore harmony.

AM: (Pronounced AHM). Toned at night, this will balance and relax your chakra system and lead to a peaceful sleep/dreamtime.

How does toning these sounds make you feel?

_____

_____

_____

_____

_____

_____

Whether you are meditating or toning, practice makes perfect. As you use these toning methods, you will become more comfortable with them and they will feel very natural. They are! They are part of our cellular make up. "As above, so below." When you realize that our physical bodies are a microcosm of the macrocosm, you come to learn that we are indeed a part of all that is. In remembering these tones, you are simply remembering a part of your Self that is made up of very high vibration frequencies.

After toning or chanting, take a moment to feel and express what may have transpired during this high vibration state. This is called inspirational writing. By tapping into the higher realms you are able to retrieve information that may not otherwise be available to you during your hectic day. Write down everything you may have heard, seen or felt during or just after toning. Do not edit your writing; simply let it flow through you. Just as an artist lets his/her vision flow through a paintbrush, let your experience move through your pen. By letting the words flow uninterrupted by your logical mind and ego, you will have a clear account of your spiritual encounter.

Have you ever wondered about the energy of your own name, or what may have caused you to choose it for yourself prior to your physical incarnation? Our names have unique and special meanings. Like the Angels, the letters and sounds used to create our names also resonate with a sacred vibration all their own.

For example, in Celtic legend my name, Dana, represents: The Goddess Dana, whose people, the elves, were known as the Tuatha de Danaan.

According to the Celtic Ogham, the first letter of my name "D," represents the strength of the mighty oak tree. This strength is imparted to me through the energy of my name.

What does your name mean? If you don't know off hand, it's easy enough to find out by performing a search on the internet.

My name is _____ and it means:

_____

_____

_____

_____

_____

Just as you do with other forms of toning, chant your name in increments of three and then 'watch' and 'feel' how your name affects you:

My experience:

Take note of anything you felt, heard or saw while toning your name.

_____

_____

_____

_____

_____

_____

_____

"The privilege of a lifetime is being who you are. The goal of the hero trip down to the jewel point is to find those levels in the psyche that open, open, open, and finally open to the mystery of your Self being Buddha consciousness or the Christ. That's the journey."

Joseph Campbell (1904—1987), American Mythologist
"A Joseph Campbell Companion"

There is No Ending So, Let's Talk About New Beginnings

It is my wish for you, my fellow mystic, that as you continue to walk the journey of each lifetime, you do so with a sense of playfulness, awe and wonder. Remember that as one window closes, another, much clearer window opens. And in shedding our old worn out vestments, we clothe ourselves in Universal Grace.

Living our lives with a sense of divine purpose and knowing that we are fully supported by Spirit makes our life a grand adventure. The attitude with which we embark upon the adventure directs the course of our experiences and the experiences of those around us.

In walking the Mystic Journey with confidence, forgiveness and with a light heart, we teach others to do the same.

May each of us leave a trail of Enlightenment, Happiness, Truth and Love, for generations of Mystics yet to come.

P.S. One Last Thing About the Light

"You're my Angel on earth."

That's what I tell my dearly loved friend, Sister Irene.

Her dancing green eyes and lively auburn hair, decorate a face that, to me, is celestial Light made flesh.

When I asked her if she would give my manuscript a final edit, as always, she readily agreed to help.

Irene knows me. She understands my Gifts and my Journey.

Aside from editing the grammar and punctuation, I asked her if she might be willing to offer some added insight. Through her lens as an earth Angel and a Roman

Catholic nun, I wondered what she might add to a book such as this one.

Here is what she had to say:

"I'm thinking you should have a 'clincher.' I don't know if you'd call it Afterword or Afterthought or something more creative. This would be after your last chapter. I think it would be neat if you wrote it as though you were talking to your two kids. Even though in *real* life they probably already know this...pretending you're writing this to your kids would give your words a loving, simple tone."

"Pretend your kids ask you, "Hey, you've told me so much stuff...what can I do day to day to remain "in the light?"

"I would then talk about the importance of being grateful...for both little and big things that happen in our lives. Maybe I'd suggest keeping a Gratitude Journal to write in frequently. Then I'd briefly explain how important it is to hang out with "life giving" people. I also might mention that part of our journey in life involves looking beneath the obvious to see the *real*. And since likes attract, our own Light may help another's flickering flame to become stronger...because of our love. In other words, when we look at other people we can see them with eyes the same way God or Spirit sees them...with unconditional love. This will not always be easy...but we know what St. Catherine said about, "all the way to heaven..."

Love and Light, Irene Mary.

Dear Dane and Elyse,

All the way to heaven *is* heaven, if you wish it to be.

Create Heaven on earth by weaving a colorful tapestry, rich with true friends of every make and model. By being one in return, I guarantee that you will have more friends than you can shake a stick at.

The Golden Rule always works.

You can experience Nirvana right here and now, by traveling the road of life with an understanding that everything happens for a reason. All of our experiences, whether we perceive them as good, or bad, are actually created out of love and serve as an opportunity to grow. The pains can be very excruciating; but don't be afraid to grow!

The sun shines most brightly right after a storm.

Decorate your Paradise on earth with a garden full of brightly colored, and sweet smelling flowers. May each fragrant blossom represent a time in your life when you gave of yourself unconditionally. Remember that each time you give, your garden grows tenfold in return. Imagine the rainbows you will create by watering your garden with giggles and laughter.

Don't forget to play!

When you realize that you are a reflection of God, and every person you meet is too, Cloud Nine will be within your reach. God is love. Therefore, *you* are, too.

God loves you just the way you are. So do I.

Perfect Bliss will arrive on your doorstep when your eyes begin to see beyond what 'appears' to be right in front of you. If you allow your soul to take a deeper look at things, you will see that you are never alone. You have been provided with heavenly helpers and the endless love of your Maker to help you walk life's journey.

You are connected to all things seen and unseen.

Ecstasy will have found its home with you, when you let your own unique and beautiful Light sparkle and shimmer as only it can. Let your Light shine! In doing so, you will give others the courage to do the same. Remember, that your Light will never be diminished by helping to light another.

Your Light is eternal. You will never cease to be.

Your Dreams will become your reality, when you understand that expressing infinite love and gratitude for everything under the sun and beyond the heavens, brings to you a greater abundance than you could ever hope for.

Say "Thank you," often.

And lastly, the Pearly Gates aren't a place outside of you. Quite the opposite. They reside within you. Once you come to know this and have the courage to walk through them, you will find where heaven truly resides. Heaven is within. What is contained within you, can be created outside of you.

See your own beauty, and you will create beauty, the likes of which have never been seen.

Having said all that, it's time to get 'crack a lackin.'

The journey of life is waiting for you!

Love, Mom

"Oh, you're the best friends anybody ever had. And it's funny, but I feel as if I'd known you all the time, but I couldn't have, could I?"

~ Dorothy

"I don't see how. You weren't around when I was stuffed and sewn together, were you?"

~ Scarecrow

"And I was standing over there, rusting for the longest time."

~ Tin Woodsman

"Still, I wish I could remember, but I guess it doesn't matter anyway. We know each other now, don't we?"

~ Dorothy

"We do."

~ Tin Woodsman

"To Oz?"

~ Scarecrow

"To Oz."

~ Tin Woodsman

Memorable Quotes from The Wizard of Oz (1939)

With Love and Infinite Gratitude

Before our birth, in the casting call to find those who will play an intricate roll in the theatre of our lives, we embrace a panorama of souls who are willing to take part in our earth Journey as family members, friends, co-workers, teachers, fellow travelers, earth angels, adversaries and soul mates. We find even furry souls, feathered souls and souls that swim, all willing to participate in creating the tapestry of our lives.

It is with humble gratitude that I thank my fellow cast members:

Mary Ann Sabo	Editor, Dear Friend, Journalist, and Founder of the Sabo Supper Club Where the Laughter Goes on Into the Early Hours.
Sister Irene Mary	Editor, Earth Angel and Someone Who Prays for Me a Whole Lot. Thank Goodness. She Teaches Me that God Has a Great Sense of Humor.
Wendy Mersman	Artist Extraordinaire Who Can Create Beauty and Laughter from the Musings of My Mind.
Mrs. Darling	Earth Angel and My Georgia Adoption Case Worker. Even Though I Don't See Her as I Grow up, I'm Quite Certain God Gave Her a Beautiful Smile and a Warm Sense of Humor, So That She Could Take Good Care of the Kids that She Assigned Her to Deliver to Their Adoptive Parents.
Mrs. Shiebly	My 5th Grade English Teacher, Who Introduces Me to the Wonders of C.S. Lewis and, "The Lion, The Witch and the Wardrobe." She Doesn't Smile Much on the Outside, but She Sure Seems to Have a Lovely Smile on the Inside. You Can Feel it When She is Reading to Her Students.

Mom and Dad	Crow and the Sarge – Not Your Average June and Ward Cleaver. Let's Just Say, They Get More Humorous with Age. Ha!
Dane Andrew Iwaniw	My Son Who Makes Me Very Proud by Being Who He Is: A Very Old Soul Who is Intelligent, Loving, Funny, Protective, Athletic, Kinda Grumpy, and a Self Proclaimed Momma's Boy. Sometimes We Laugh Until We Can Hardly Breathe.
Elyse Marie LaFave Iwaniw	My Free Spirited, Horse Loving, Fearless and Compassionate Daughter, Who Reminds Me Constantly that Life is for Living and that Bulls were Given Horns so that We Could Grab them! She Laughs so Hard, Her Eyes Water and She Snorts Out Loud. Listening to Her Makes Me Do the Same.
Tim Cronk	My Little Brother Who Makes Me Crazy and Makes Me Laugh Harder than Anyone Else on Earth.
Steve Iwaniw	Hands down, the Best at Telling Funny Stories or Making Ordinary Stories Sound Funny. He's Part of the Reason Adults Need Disposable Underwear.

Michael, Angela, Nik, Blake, Tim, Katie, Scott, Sarah, Andrew and Anna

	My Nieces and Nephews Who Bless Me with Their Youthful Wisdom, Laughter, Hugs, and emails. They Honor Me with the Privilege of Watching Them Blossom Into the Beautiful and Loving Spirits that They Are.
Skyler Kay	My Free Spirited Niece Who Looks Like a Faerie Princess and Likes to Tell Me that I am Her Favorite Auntie. One Day She will Tell Me this Without My Coaching Her to do So.

Sonia Choquette	Remarkable Teacher, Author and the Person Who Gives Me a Much Needed Kick in the Cosmic Butt. She Reminds Me to Laugh Along the Psychic Pathway.
Darlene Frederick	School Mate, Kindred Spirit, Life Time Friend and Traveling Buddy. She Brings Clean Underwear to the Hospital for Me (without complaining out loud). We Laugh in the Face of Adversity, Unruly Children, Stupid Stuff and Usually Over a Glass of Really Good Chardonnay.
Linda Miller	My Friend with an Unconditional Heart and Penchant for Younger Men. We laugh a *lot*; Particularly at Sabo Supper Club Dinners.
Ruthie	Wonderful Friend with a Spicy Attitude and a Love for the Windy City. We Laugh a Lot over Martinis and Butternut Squash Soup.
Mrs. Schoemaker	My Friend and Roomie, "Ruby", Who Introduces Me to World Travel and the Need for Lavender Essential Oils and Extra Toilet Paper when Going Oversees. We Laugh about a Whole Lot of Stuff that Others Might Not Find Funny.
John Davis	My Coptic Brother and Prototype of Humble Service to Humanity. He Calls Himself the "Joy Policeman" and Doesn't Think He's Funny. John Should Arrest Himself for the Joy and Laughter He Brings Others.
Jeanna Billings	My Friend Who Teaches Me that Animals Really Do Talk, and is Willing to Drink Tea with Me, Dressed in a Feathered Hat and Boa: In Public. We Laugh all the Time, even When We're in our Regular Clothes.

Rita Corn	My Friend who Teaches Me and Others that Laughter is a Healing Vibration.
Gregory & Cynthia	My Friends who Get Married in Camelot, and Ask Me to Perform the Ceremony. We Laugh a Lot Over Donut Bank Donuts *and* Talk into the Wee Hours of the Morning.

Raven Thunder Wolf Society – Jeanna, Tara, Beckie, Cheryl, Pam, Jackie, Darlene, Kire, Su, Brenda, Tammy, Lesley, Pamela

My Sisters of the Sacred Circle. They Understand that Laugher and Joy are the Highest Form of Reverence to Unci Maka and Tunkashila.

Carlo and Laurie Tonon	Canadian Friends Who Save My Life in the Tomb of Thutmosis IV, in the Valley of the Kings, Egypt. We Laugh about it a Few Days After it Happens. It Isn't Really Funny at the Time.
Bee	Loves Me Just the Way I Am.
Denise Mason	The Friend that I Have to Travel All the Way to England to Meet, Although She Lives Just Miles Away. Not Only Does She Make People Beautiful on the Outside, She Reminds Them of How Beautiful They are on the Inside, Too. Laughing and Swimming in the Ocean at Tintagel is Forever Etched in My Memory.

E'Po	Hawaiian Surfing Instructor, Who Reminds Me that When the Ocean of Life Hands Me a Big Wave that Dashes Me Into the Rocks, I Must Get Up on My Board, Ride the Surf Again and Learn to Laugh at the Bruises.

Chief and Medicine Man, Wakinyan Sna Mani, Pine Ridge Reservation, SD
Kindred Spirit Who Welcomes Me Home to the Lakota People. He Encourages and Creates Sacred Laughter in the Inipi.

Mett	My Friend with Unshakeable Faith in the Unseen Mysteries. She is very, very funny. (Funny haha, not funny odd).
Students and Clients	Friends, Kindred Spirits, Providers of Inspiration and Laughter. They are My Teachers and Cheer Leaders Along the Journey
Mother and Father God	Creative Genius and Casting Director. The Supreme Creator of Laughter and Light.

Denise Iwaniw

A native of Georgia, Denise and her family now live in Michigan. A medium of international renown, she gives private readings and workshops to men, women and children from around the world. Denise teaches classes and workshops both internationally and in the U.S., in a wide variety of areas, including Reiki, paths to spiritual enlightenment and psychic development.

You can visit Denise on her website at: www.templewithin.com

Also from Denise Iwaniw
and
The Temple Within Publishing:

Meditations from The Temple Within
Journaling Workbook and Guided Meditation CD
A Guide to Meeting Your Angels, Spirit Guides & Connecting to the
Voice of Your Higher Self

*

The Athlete Within—Accessing Your Energy Source
Guided Visualization CD for student and professional athletes as well as practitioners
of energy movement to access and balance their internal energy source
"Take your game and your workout to a whole new level."

*

Beyond the Veil Lies... a Mystic Journey—The Meditations
Guided Meditation CD
Taken from her 2004 journey to Cornwall, England, this is a CD of guided
meditations that taps into the energy of the court of Camelot
"Journey beyond the veil...to the wellspring of sacred knowledge at Glastonbury
Abbey, the Chalice Well and Merlin's Cave. Walk the Mystic's Journey to your own
Temple Within and experience the Grace in your connection to the Divine."

To order these books and cd's on-line go to: www.templewithin.com

Resources

The American Heritage College Dictionary. Boston, New York: Houghton Mifflin, 1993

The Daily Inspiration. TheDailyInspiration.com. Huntsville, AL: Future Point Communication, 2005

The Holy Bible.

183

My Personal Journal Toward Spiritual Awakening